AF594691

SALVATION

JIMMY DE SANA

PRIMARY INFORMATION

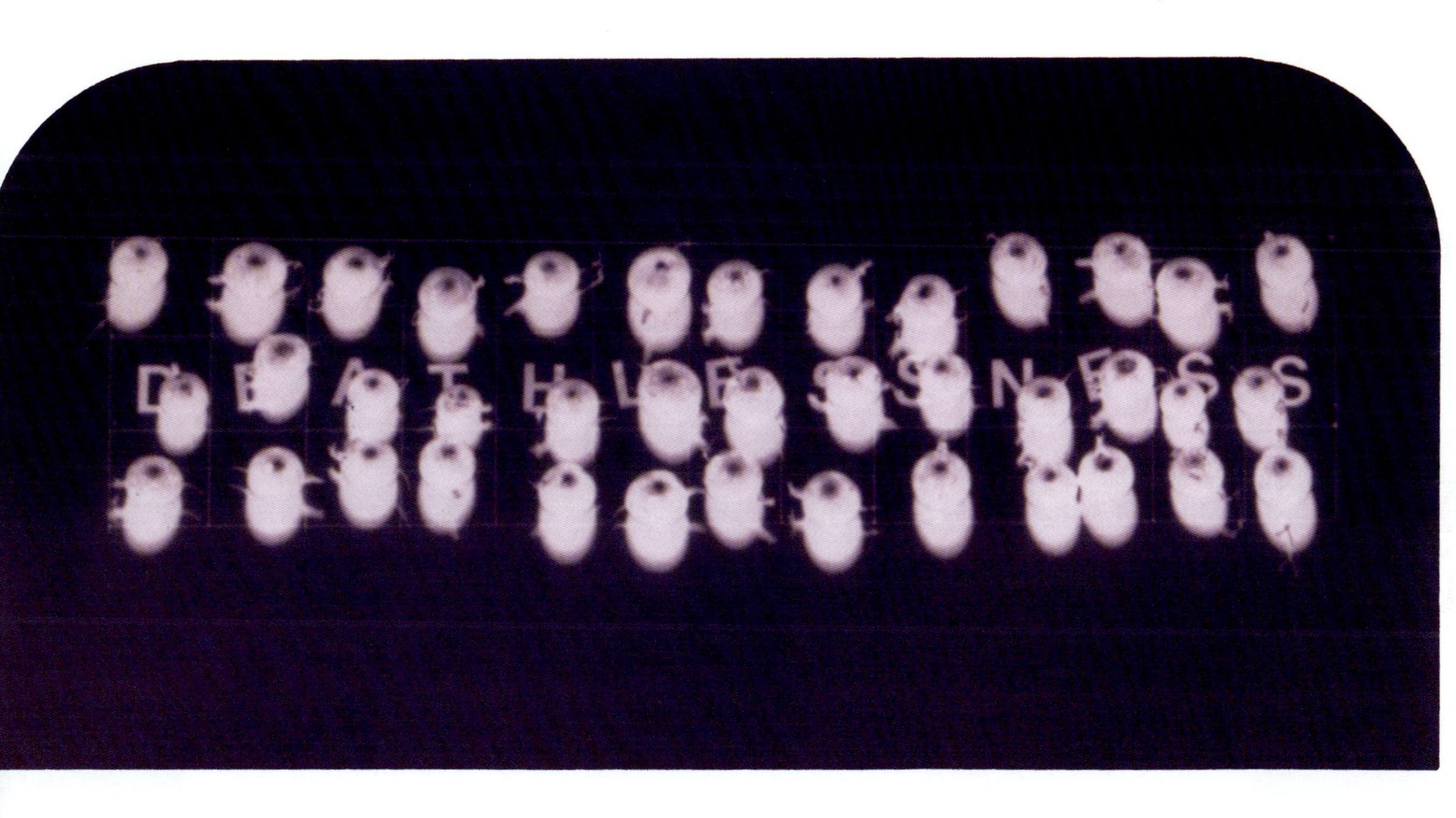
DEATHLESSNESS

JIMMY DE SANA - THE SALVATION OF POST-AIDS NEW YORK

JULIAN

四年前在美國ZOOM雜誌上看過JIMMY DE SANA的一批[illegible]S&M和DADA混合的藝術照片之[illegible]，[illegible]難忘，還把該雜誌列爲收藏品，其中一張叫PARTY PICS的作品是一個張口作痛苦狀的男子，滿牙縫間揷着牙簽更是我的酷愛。後來JIMMY告訴我那照片中人更是他一位牙醫朋友，不禁令我咄咄稱奇。

後來在美國紐約逛PAT HEARN畫廊，因爲他掛着一個最新的[illegible]而愛上了他。而且那批展品已跟他[illegible]人行動大有不同，變得有[illegible]，[illegible]的時候，我更好奇這作品會[illegible]令我[illegible]。

[illegible]一個[illegible]，JIMMY住在[illegible]的中心，在[illegible]了一所民居，和他的[illegible]和一隻黑白的DALMATIAN一起生活。我第一眼[illegible]他下[illegible]，我覺得他十分溫文[illegible]，有些DEATH IN VENICE中那個教授的味道，絕不會聯想到[illegible]。

JIMMY DE SANA[illegible]年代在ATLANTA[illegible]藝術教育，他的反叛在[illegible]已如火如荼[illegible][illegible]自然不能[illegible][illegible]BROOKLYN[illegible]雜誌及藝術家拍照。不過要在紐約[illegible]紅並非易事，他剛巧因感情方面鬧情緒，便自拍了一張裸體吊頸的照片，登在雜誌上。許多人以爲眞的有人自殺作爲藝術，而有些更局部遮蓋該照片的私處，連名作家WILLIAM BOURROGH也信以爲眞，打電話到雜誌社要了解當事人的心態。結果兩人聯絡上了，成了好友，後來WILLIAM BORROUGH更爲JIMMY第一本石破天驚的畫冊SUBMISSION寫序。

那序大意是說人找尋黑暗中的快樂，找尋肉體救贖，而我們需要見證這些。我們需要肯定了S&M，肯定這些照片背後的意義，及明白人類在SELF TORTURE和ECSTASY中釋放自己。

SUBMISSION是一本「很離頂」的圖片册，全是一九七七年至七九年紐約LEATHER BAR內各種S&M的HARDCORE照片，他送我一本，我也不敢帶出美國，駭人程度可想而知。許多人看了也以爲JIMMY是此道中人，他却很鬆容的答我：「很離怪的，你們不明白在AIDS之前，這種活動統治了紐約夜幕下的活動。」

「我把這些戲劇化的S&M紀錄下來，反映出紐約的OBSESSION。因爲很有噱頭，所以有人肯爲此出書。我現在想出一本彩色照片集，反而十分艱難。」他嘆氣說。

到了八三年，他做了一系列題名爲FAT的照片，是一些自己體內塞脹的自拍像，反映出美國社會一種現象——OBSESSION WITH DIETING。他喜歡用超級市場買回來的東西做道具，例如保鮮紙、錫紙、膠帶和膠紙，那股濃烈的FETISH味道表現出紐約物質生活的荒誕和顚狂。

PAT HEARN畫廊的負責人說JIMMY DE SANA比ROBERT MAPPLETHROPE更有趣，更有深度（紐約目前最紅的攝影藝術家自然是ROBERT MAPPLETHROPE，但我覺得這跟他的名人攝影對象，他在CLUB SCENE中的高調和他對黑人男性裸體的崇拜有關。但他缺乏耐人尋味、多面性和探討性，SLICK得可以。），將這兩人相提並論很有趣，而PAT HEARN的話我認爲頂不錯，因爲JIMMY的照片不僅反映出超現實味道、紐約生活方式的OBSESSION，而且更表達出

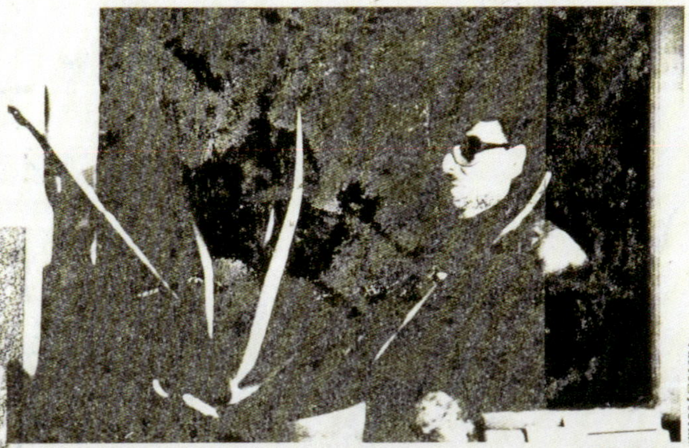

PHOTO□JULIAN

JIMMY DE SANA

HK CITY MAGAZINE, JULY 88

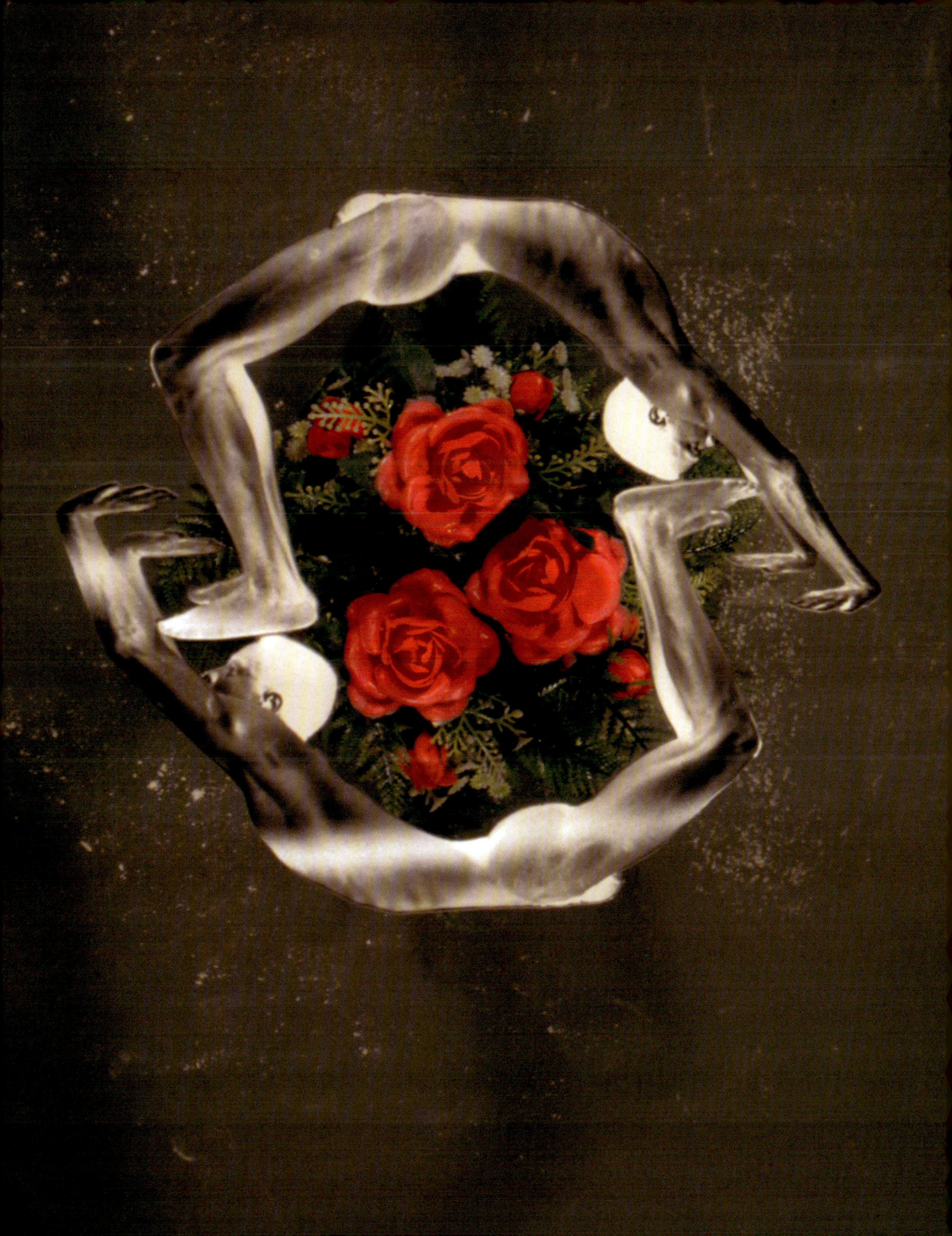

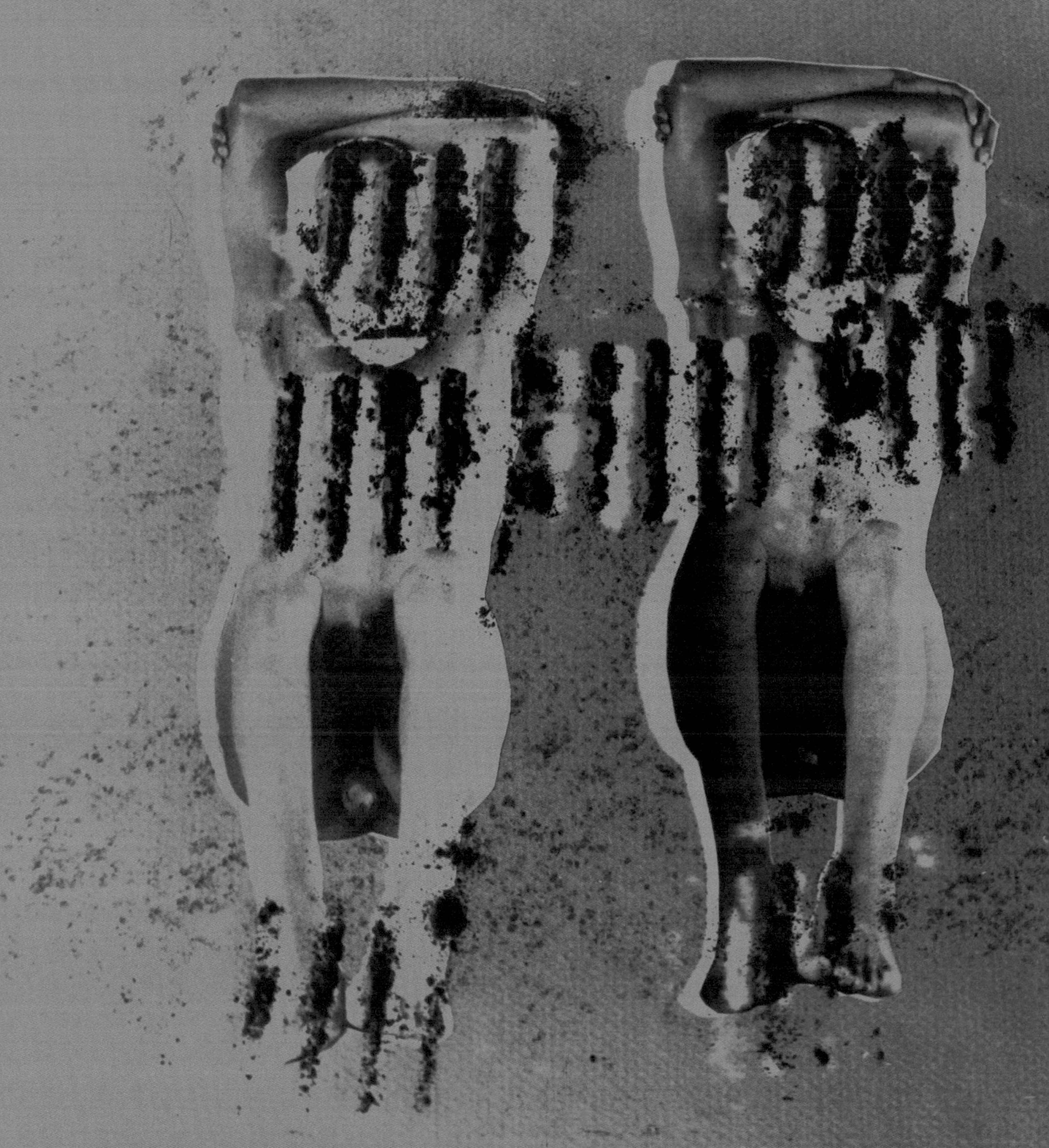

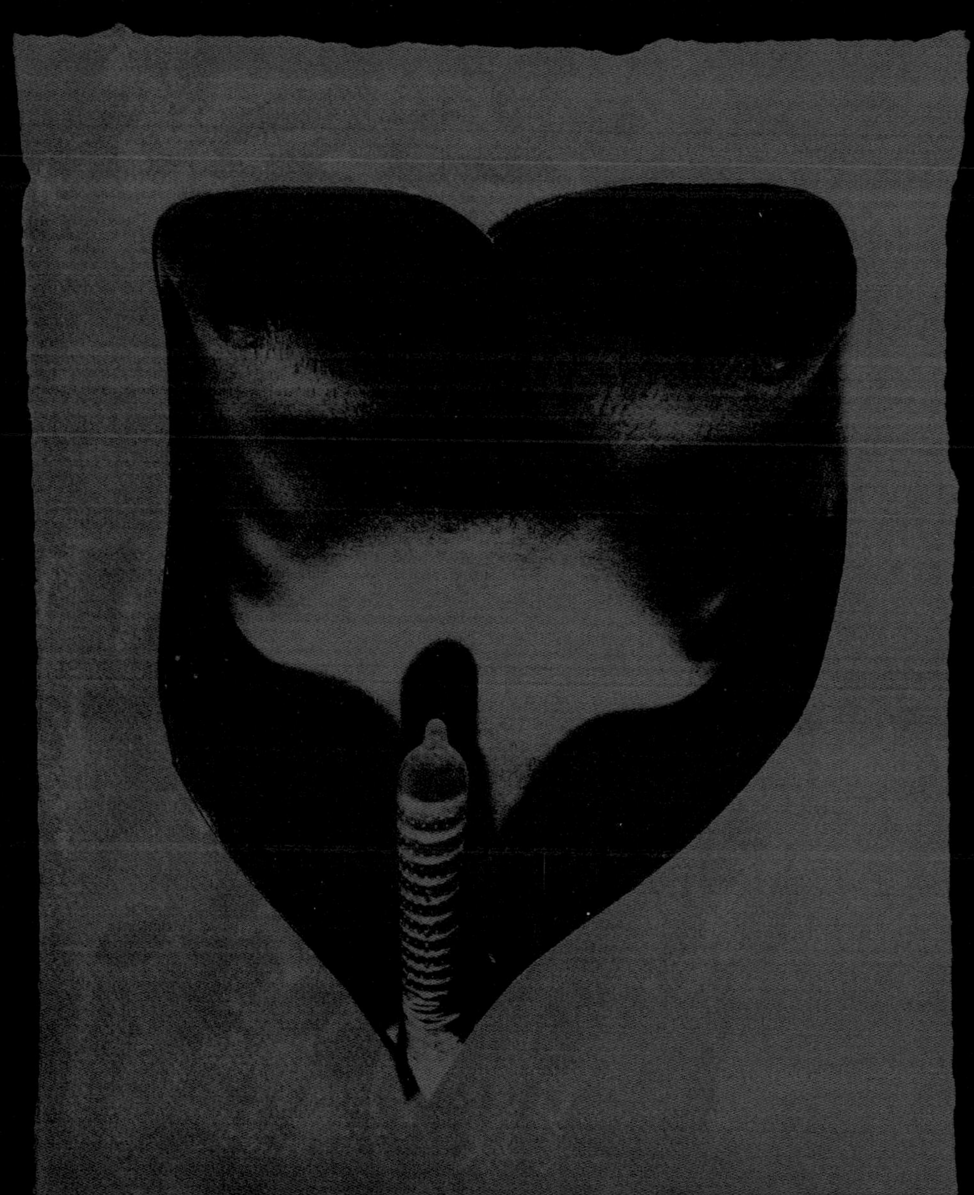

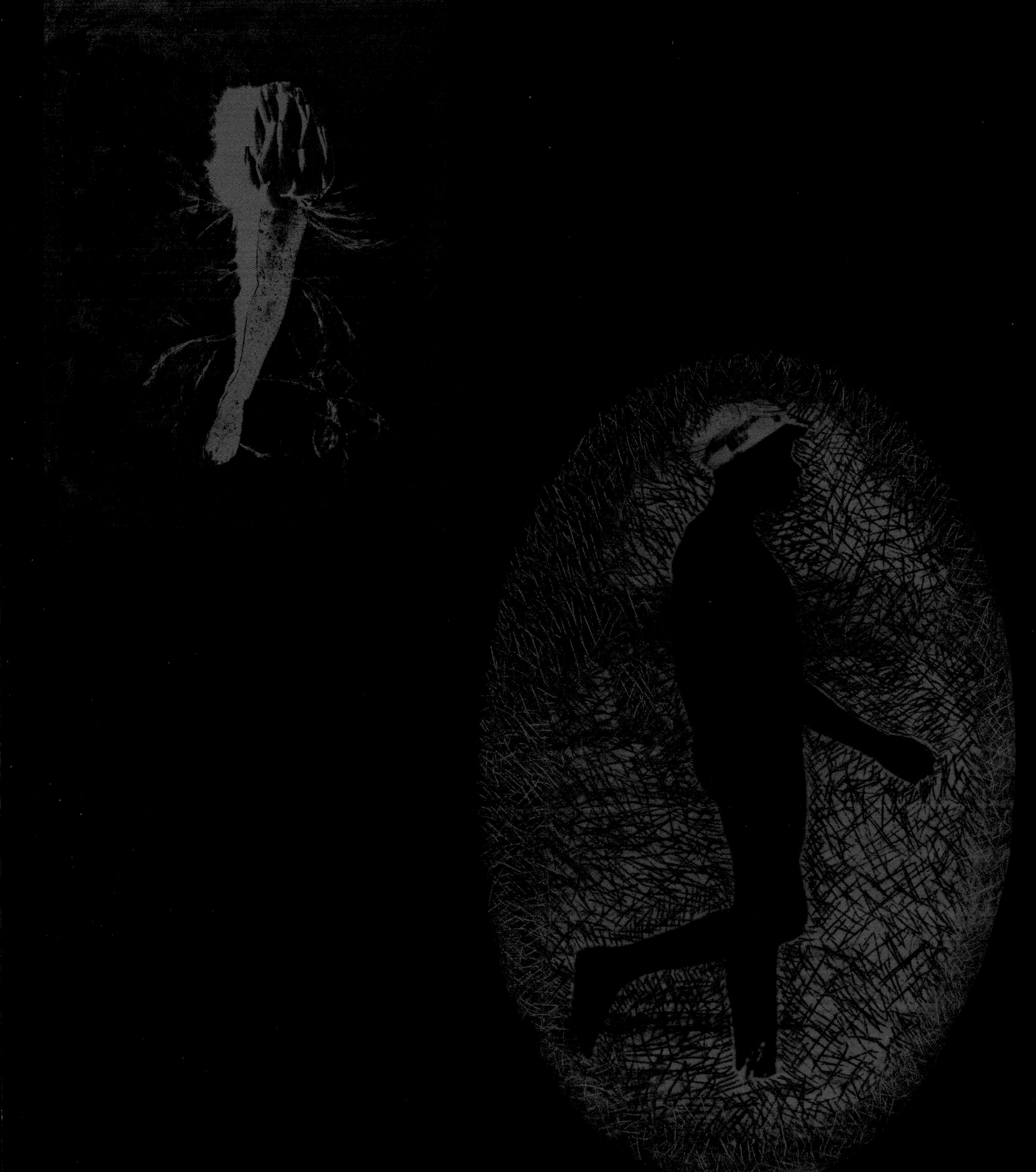

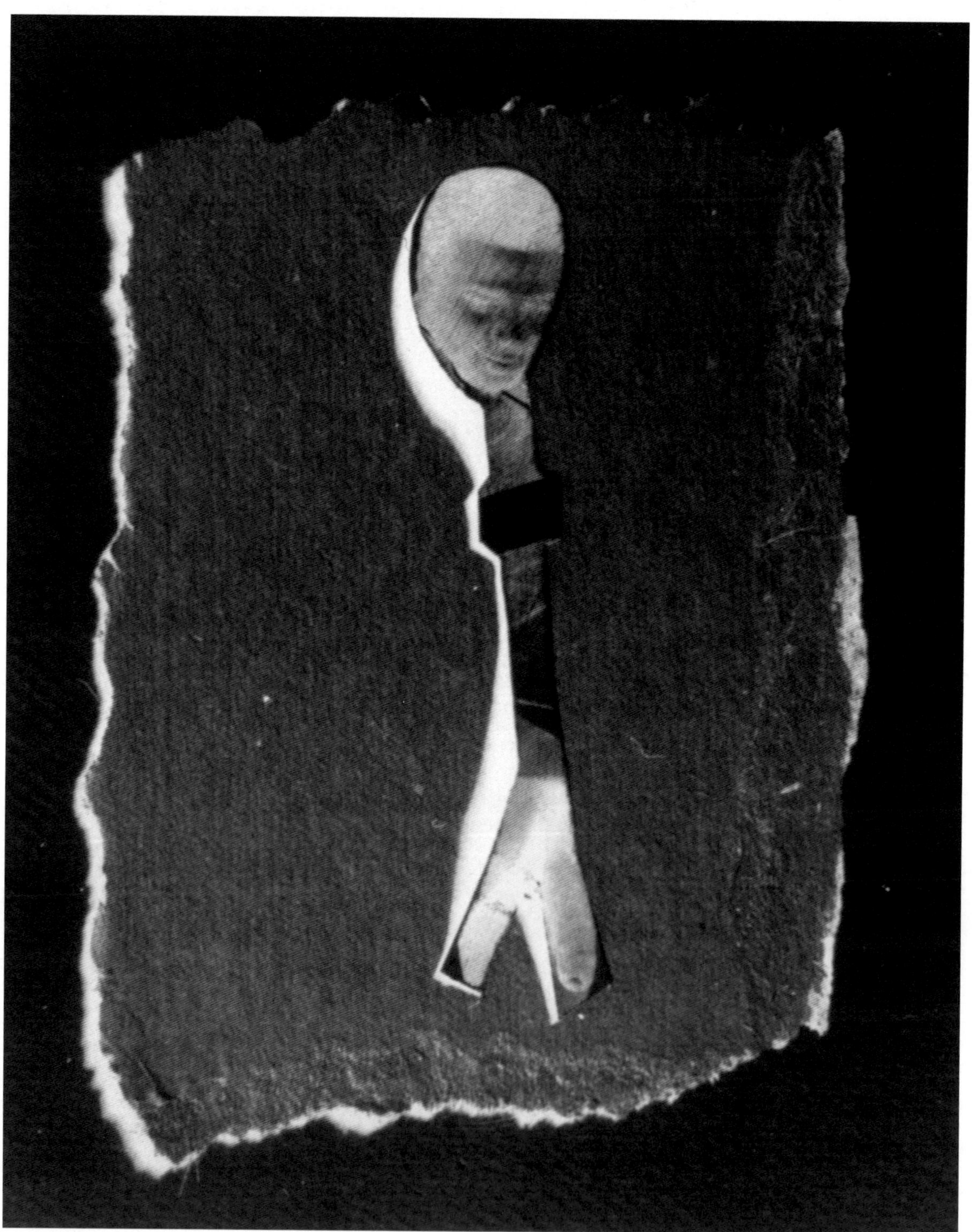

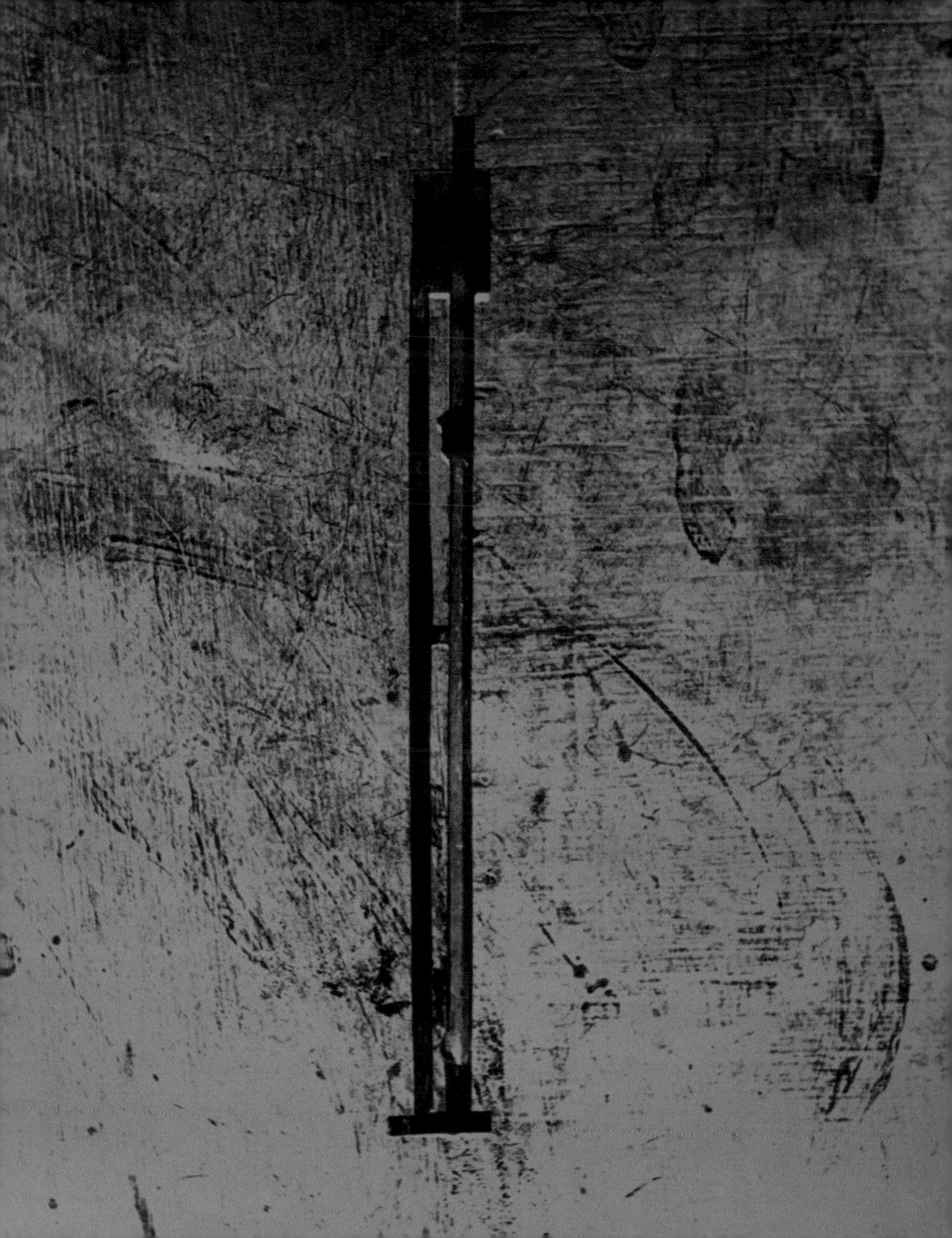

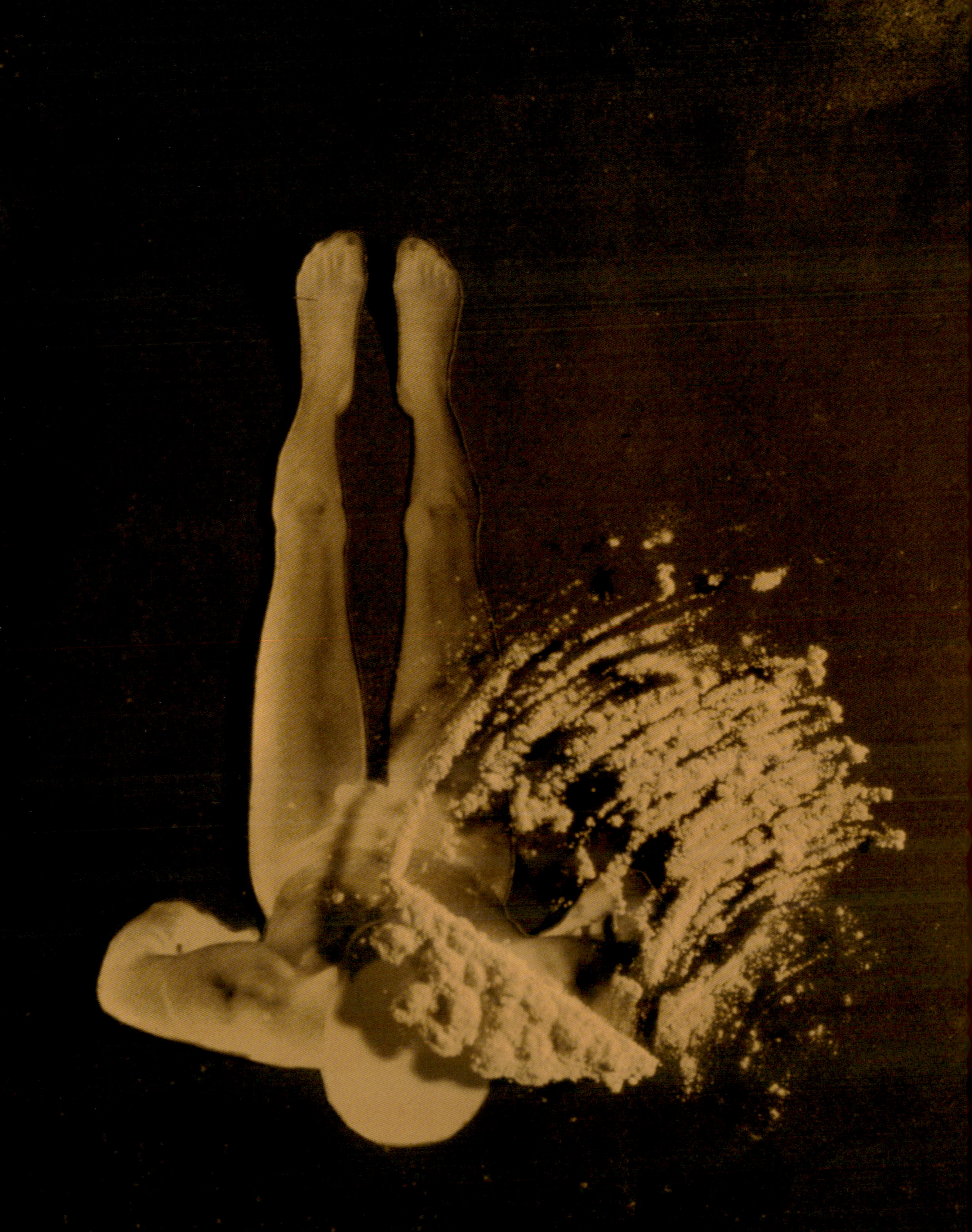

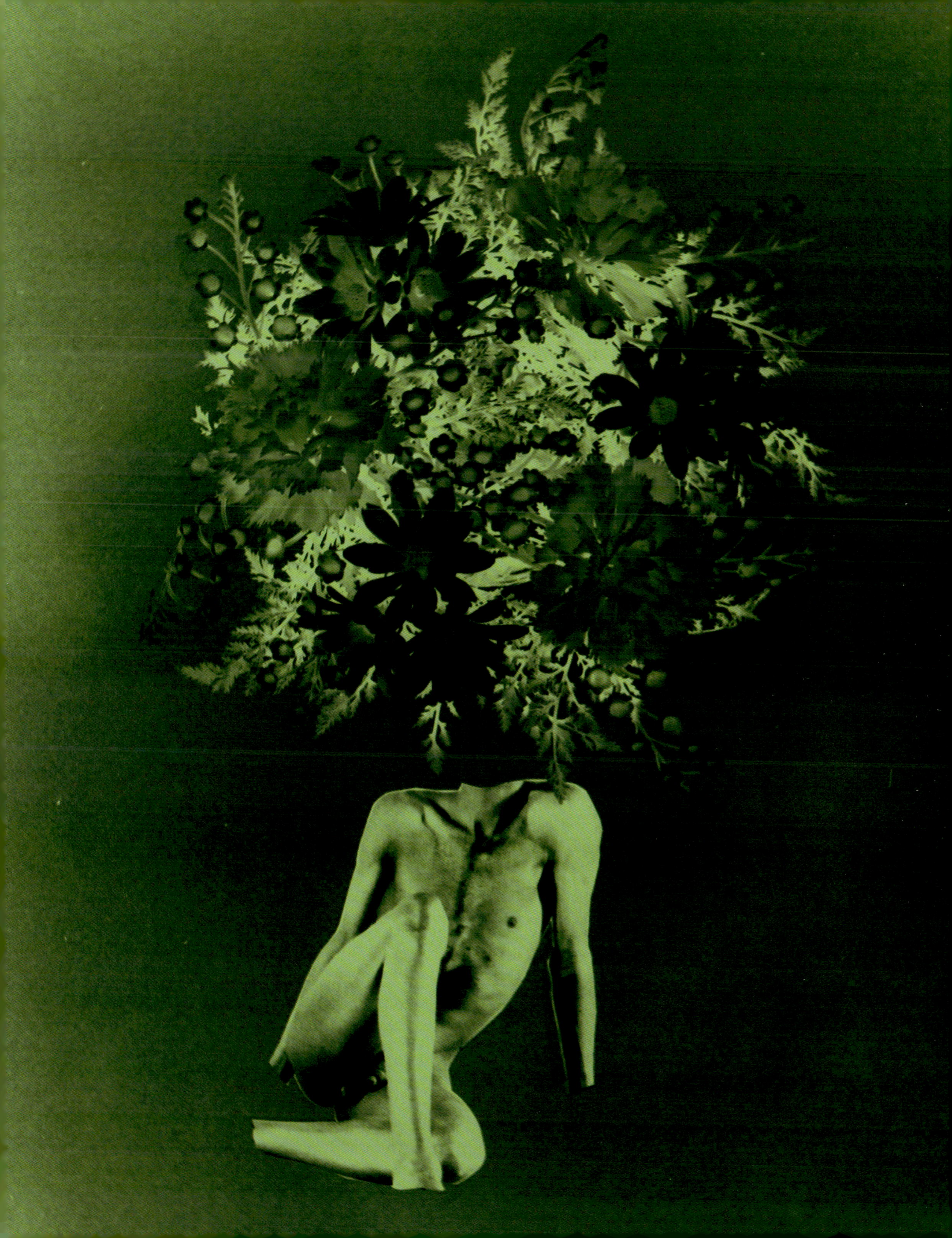

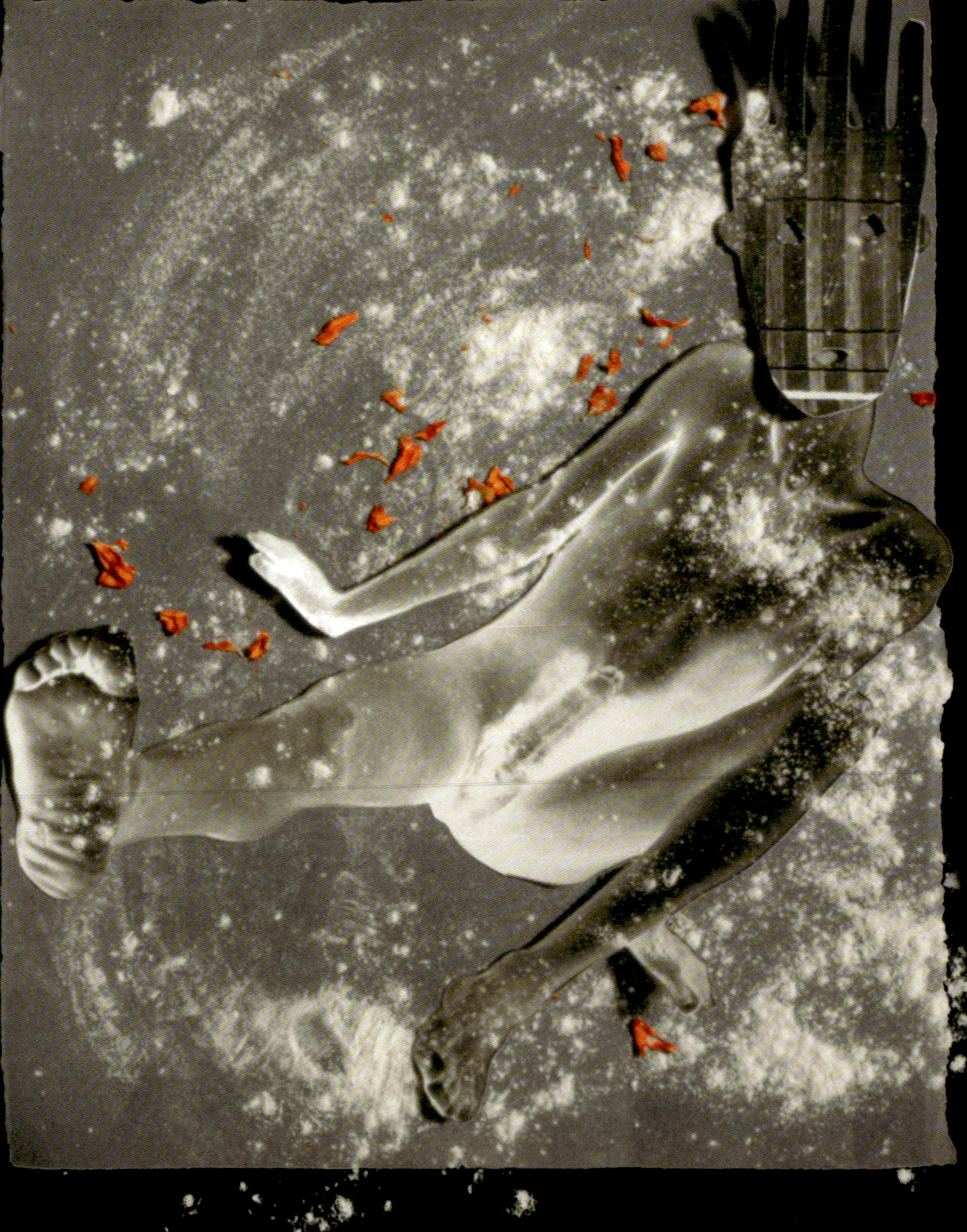

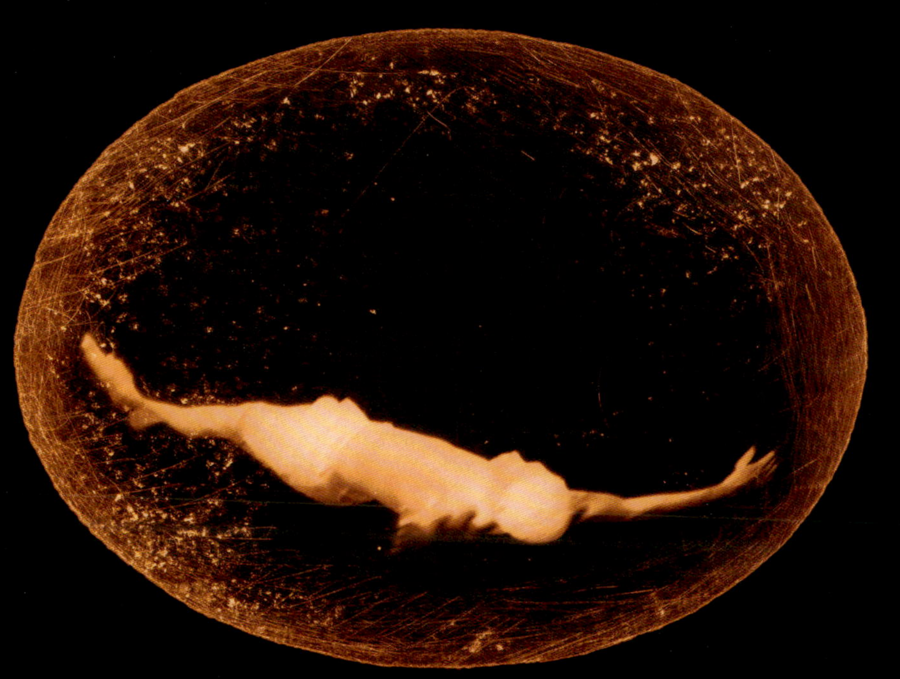

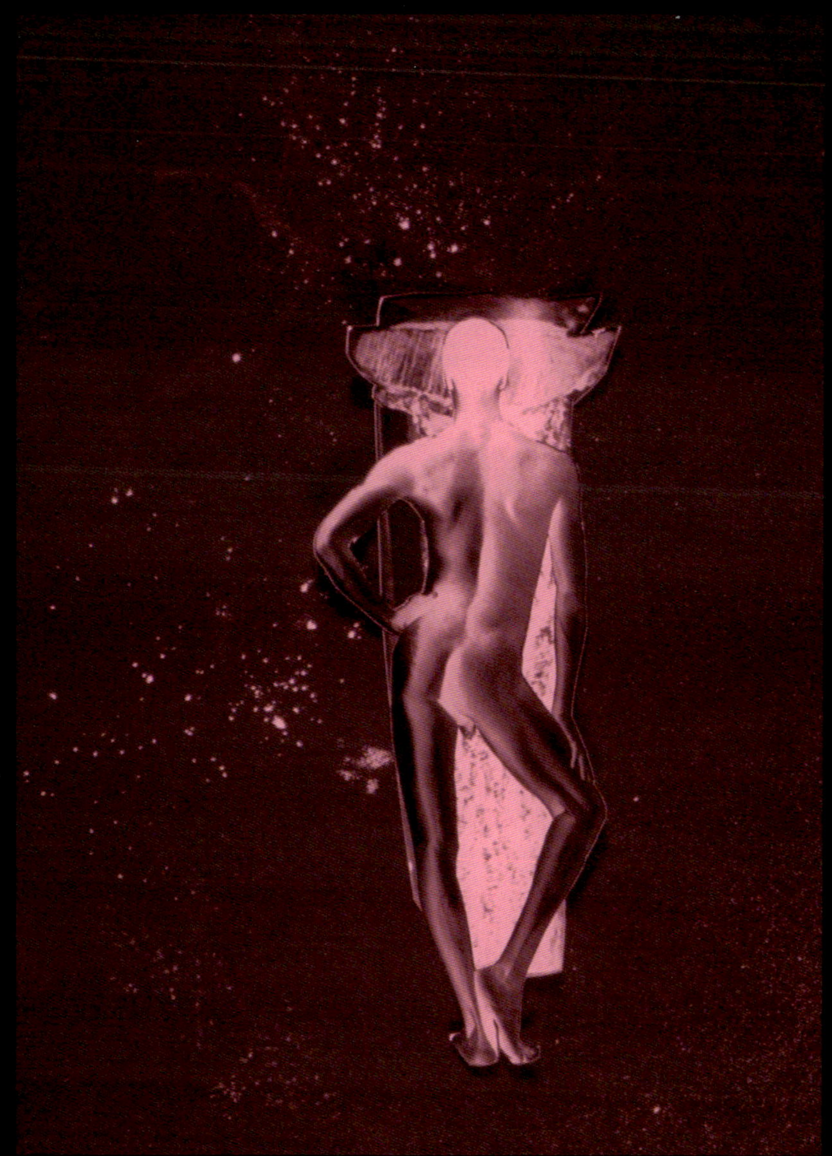

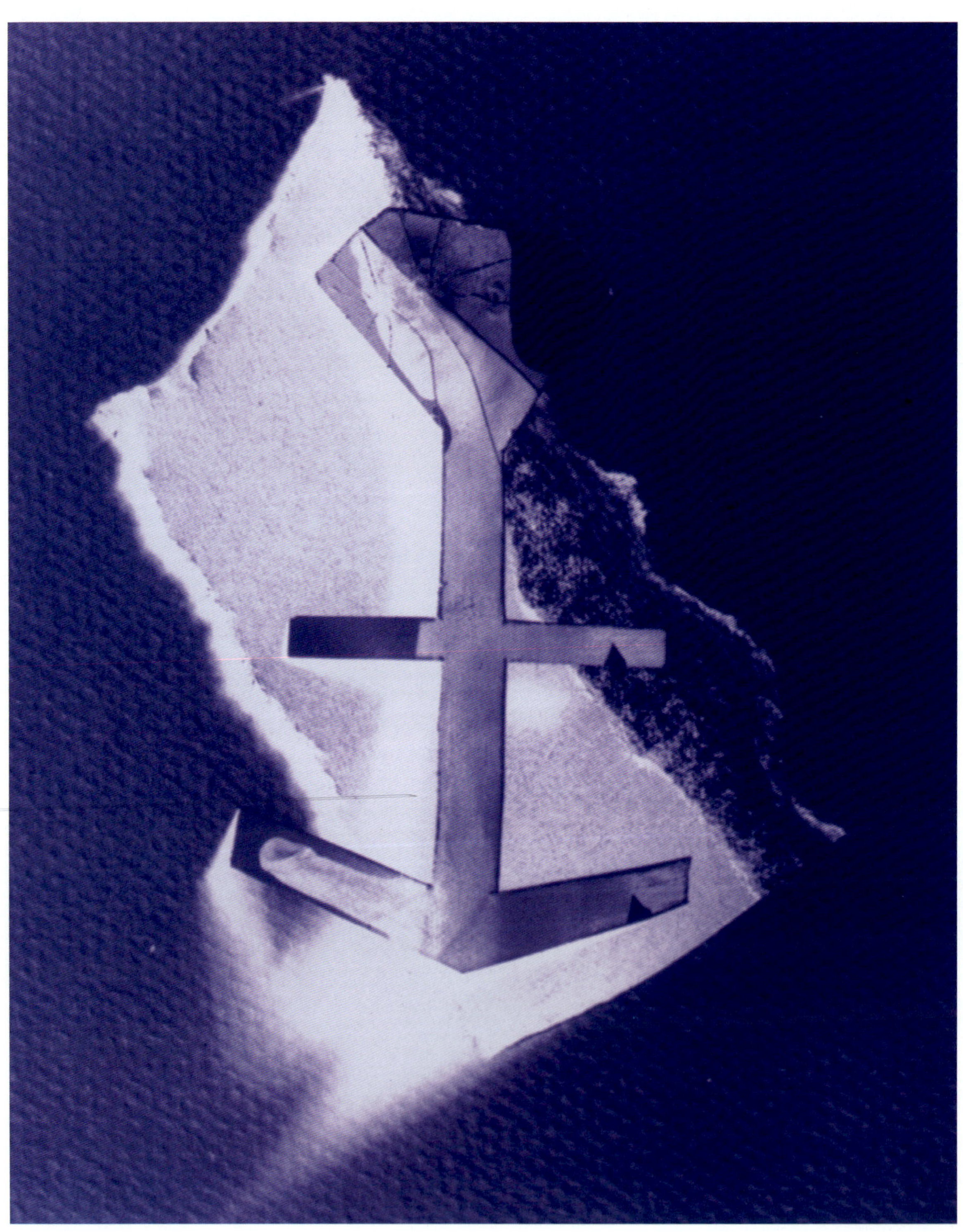

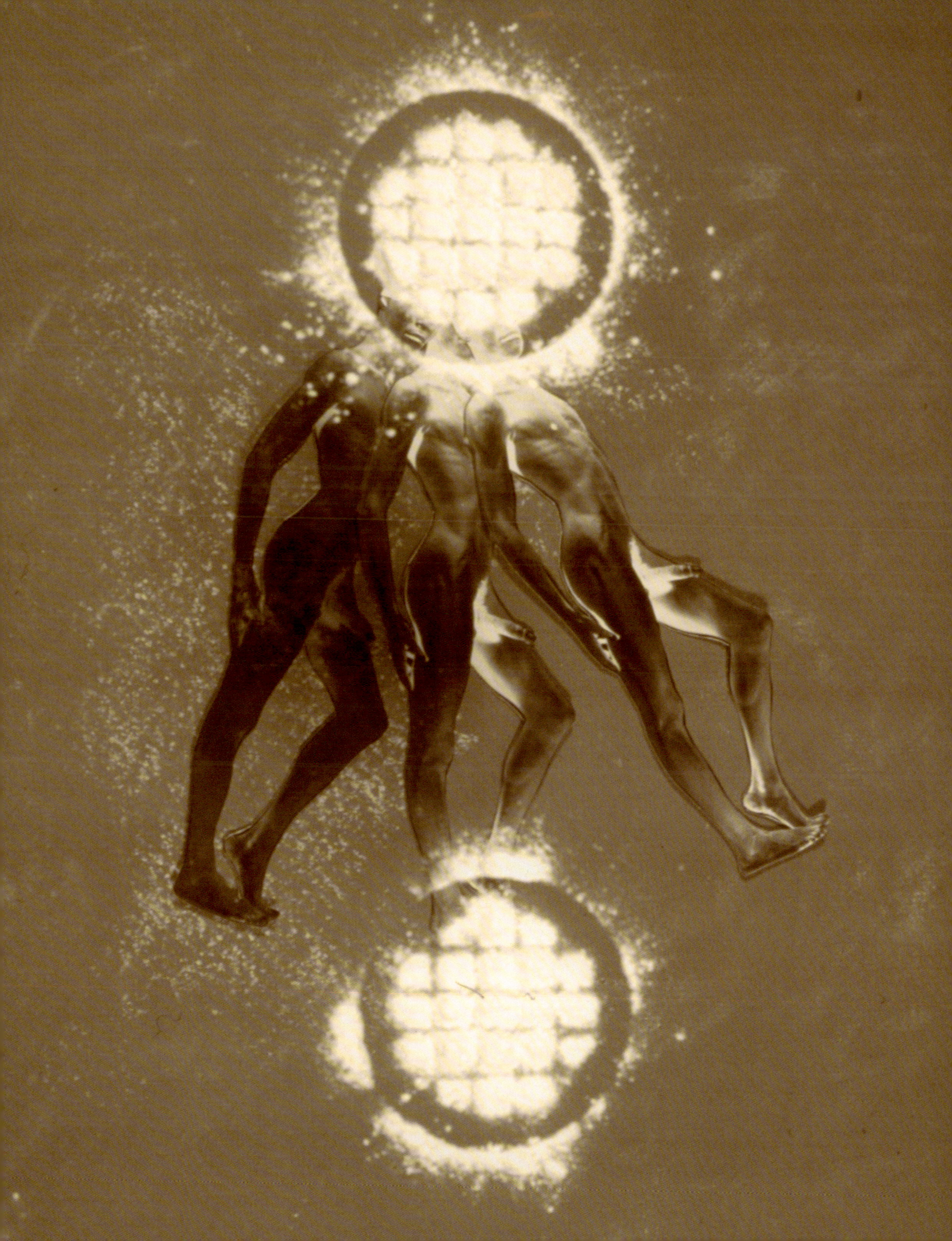

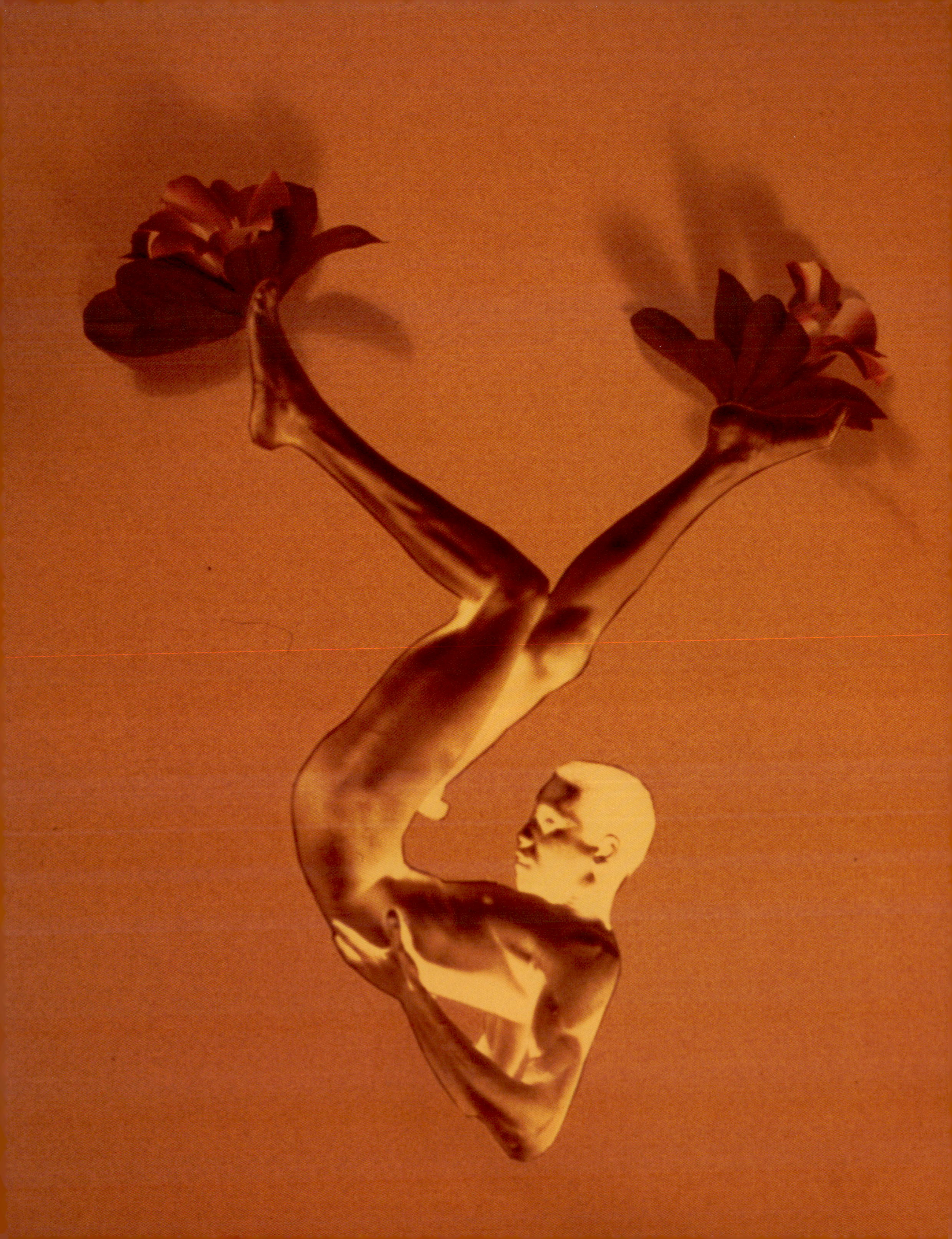

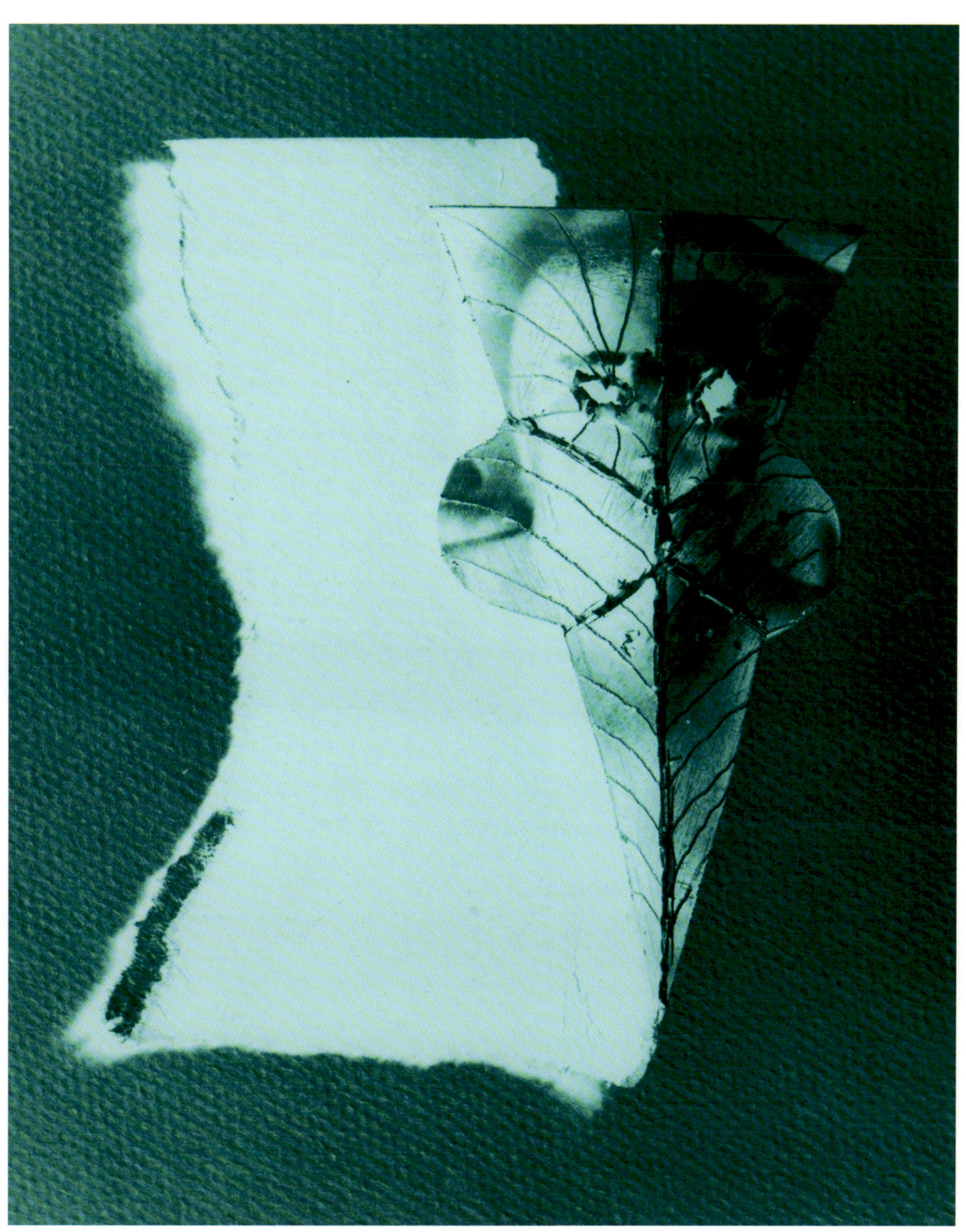

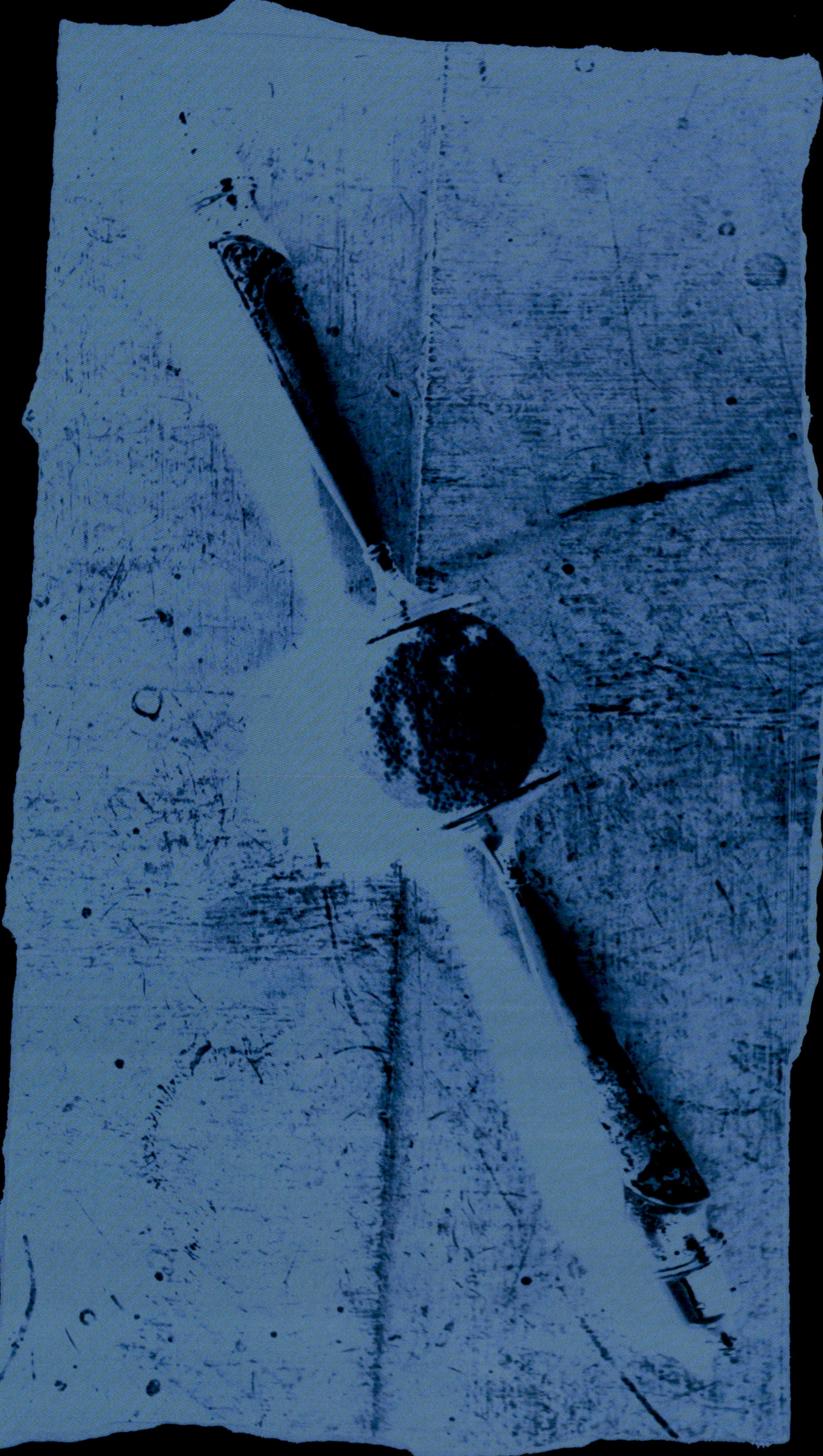

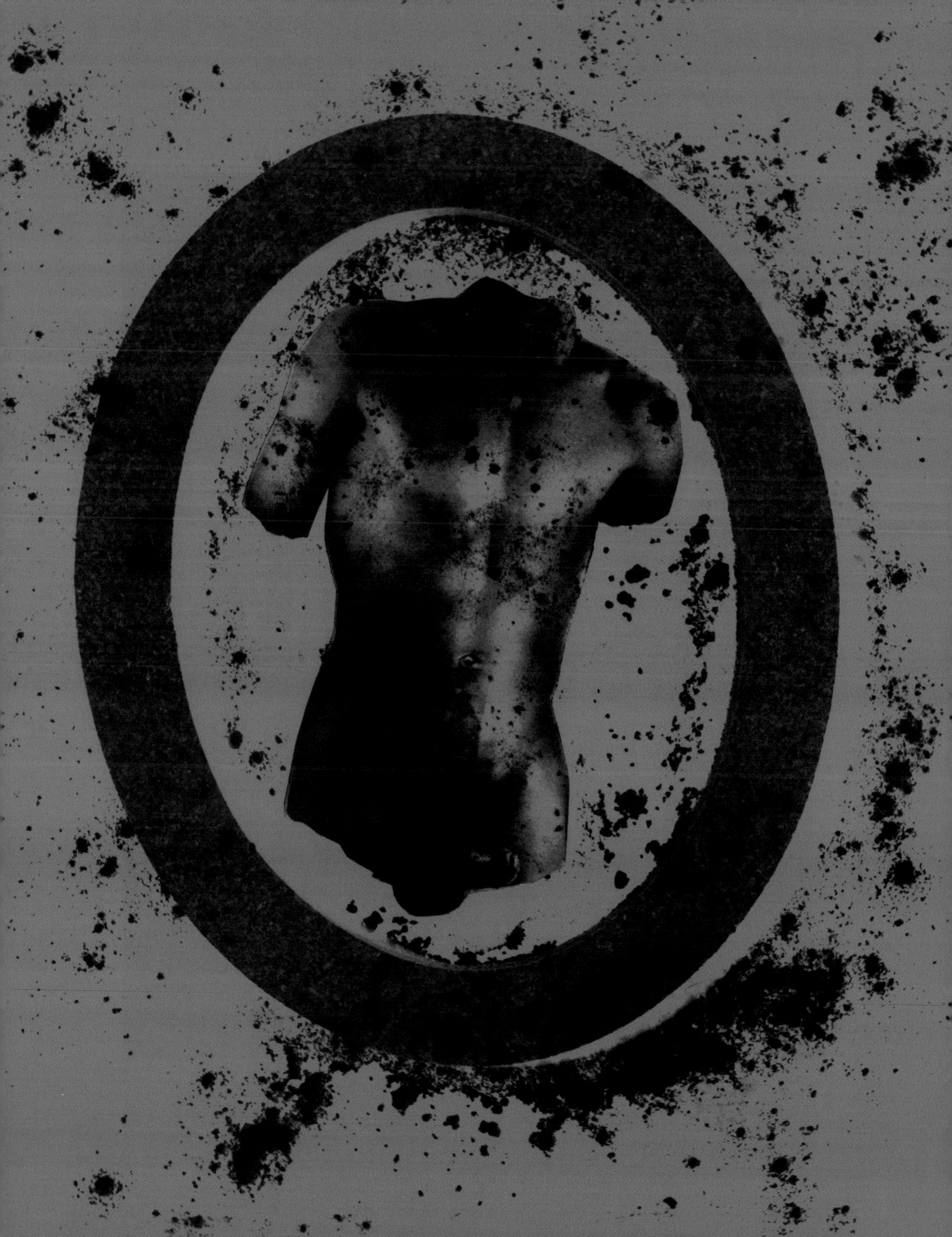

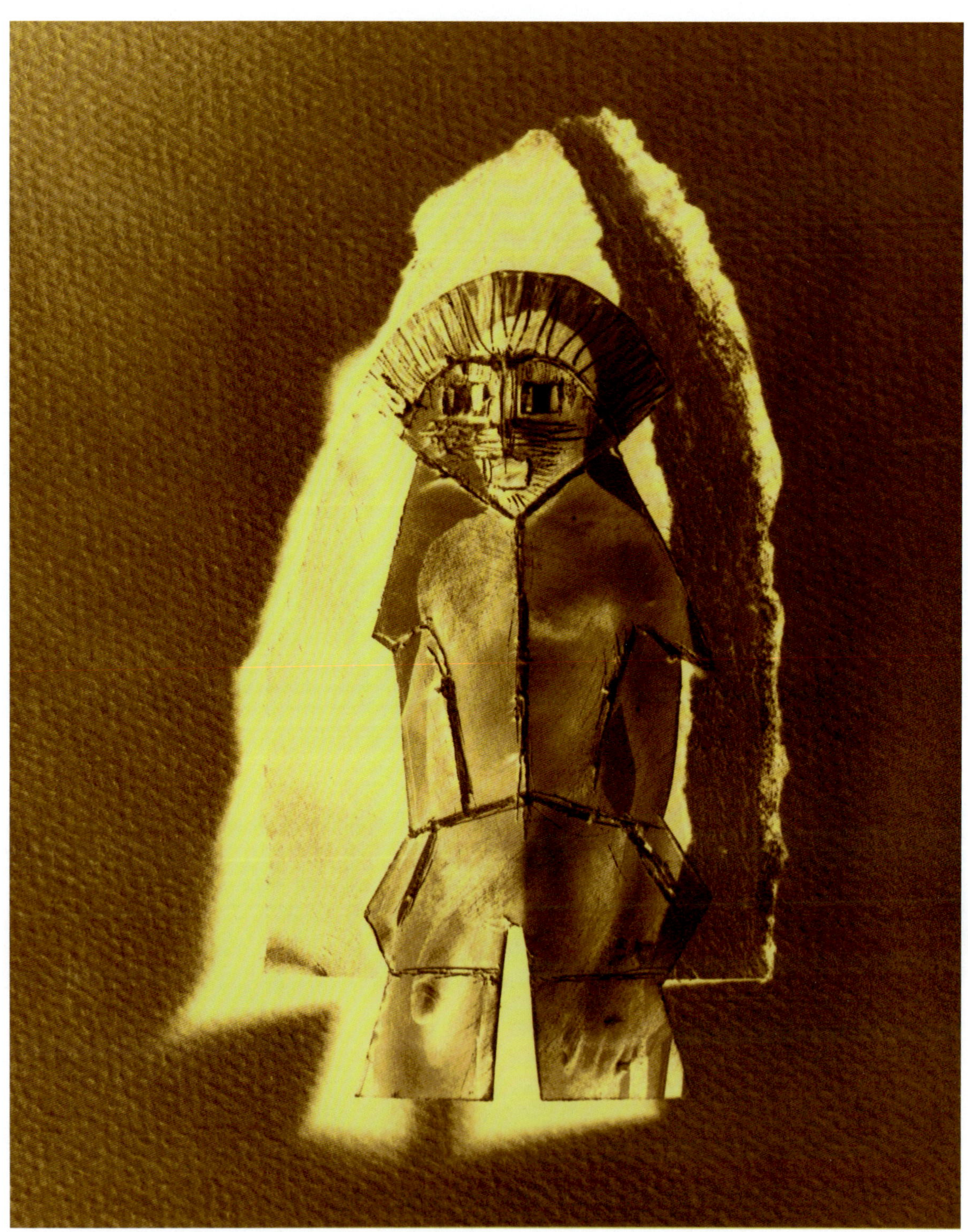

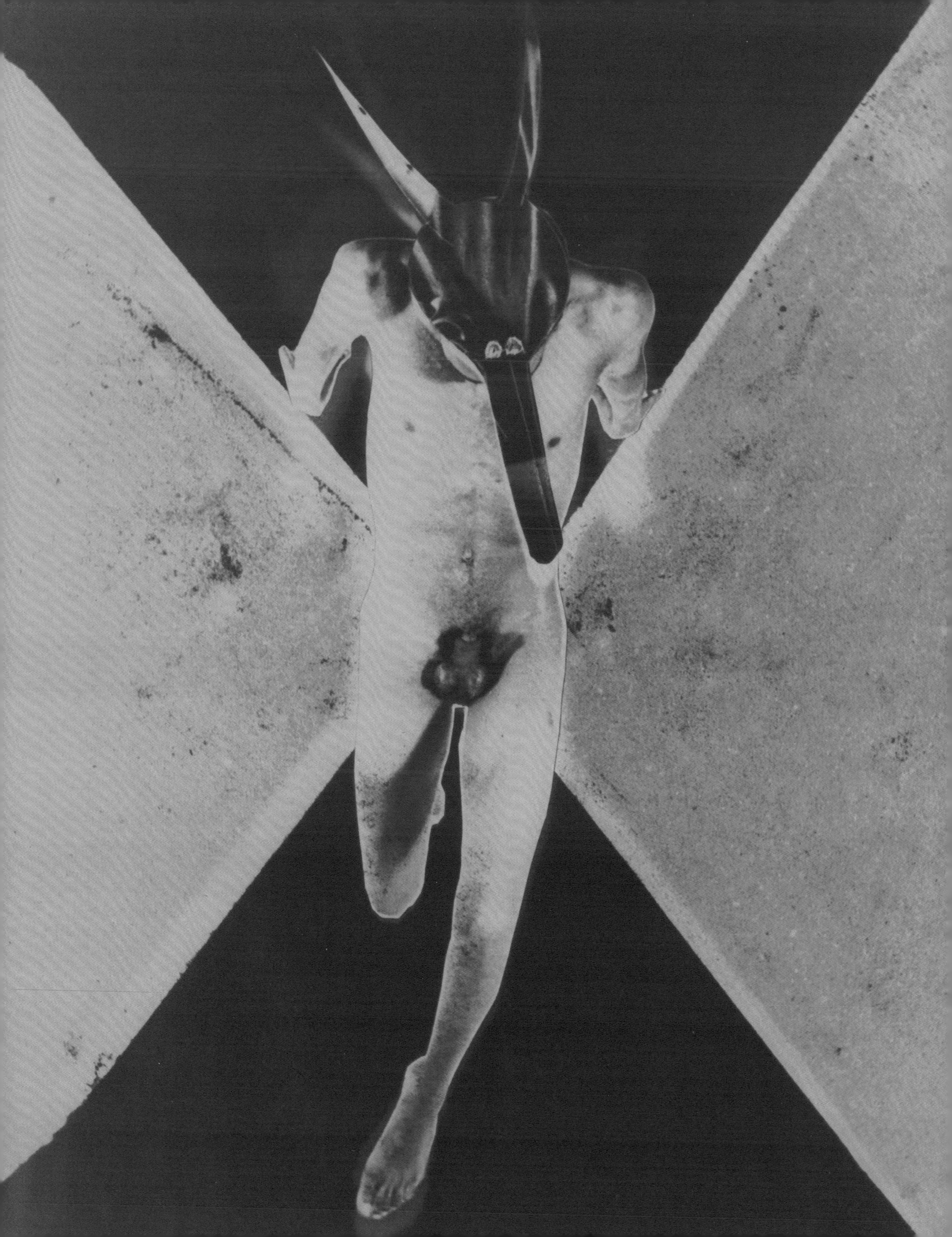

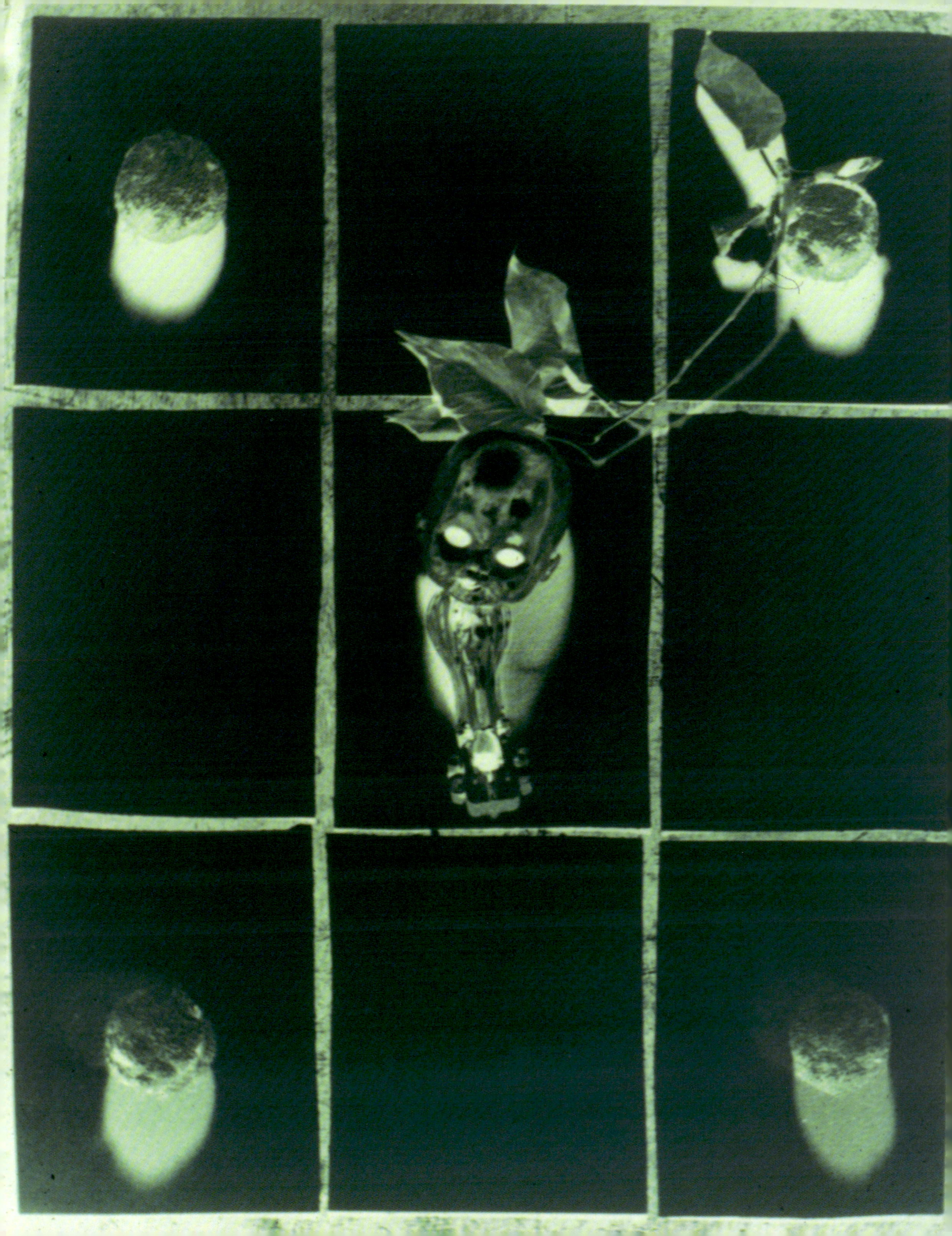

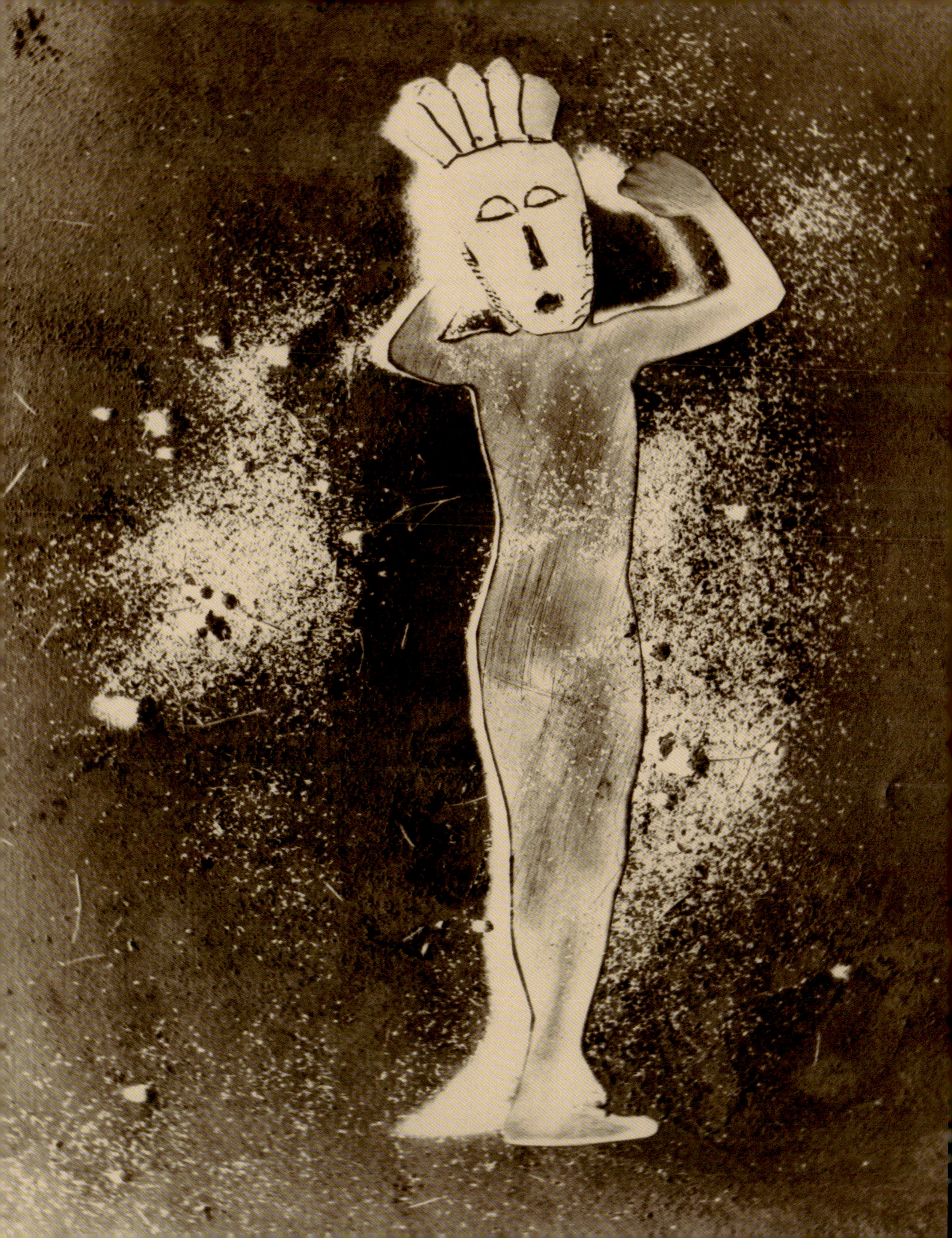

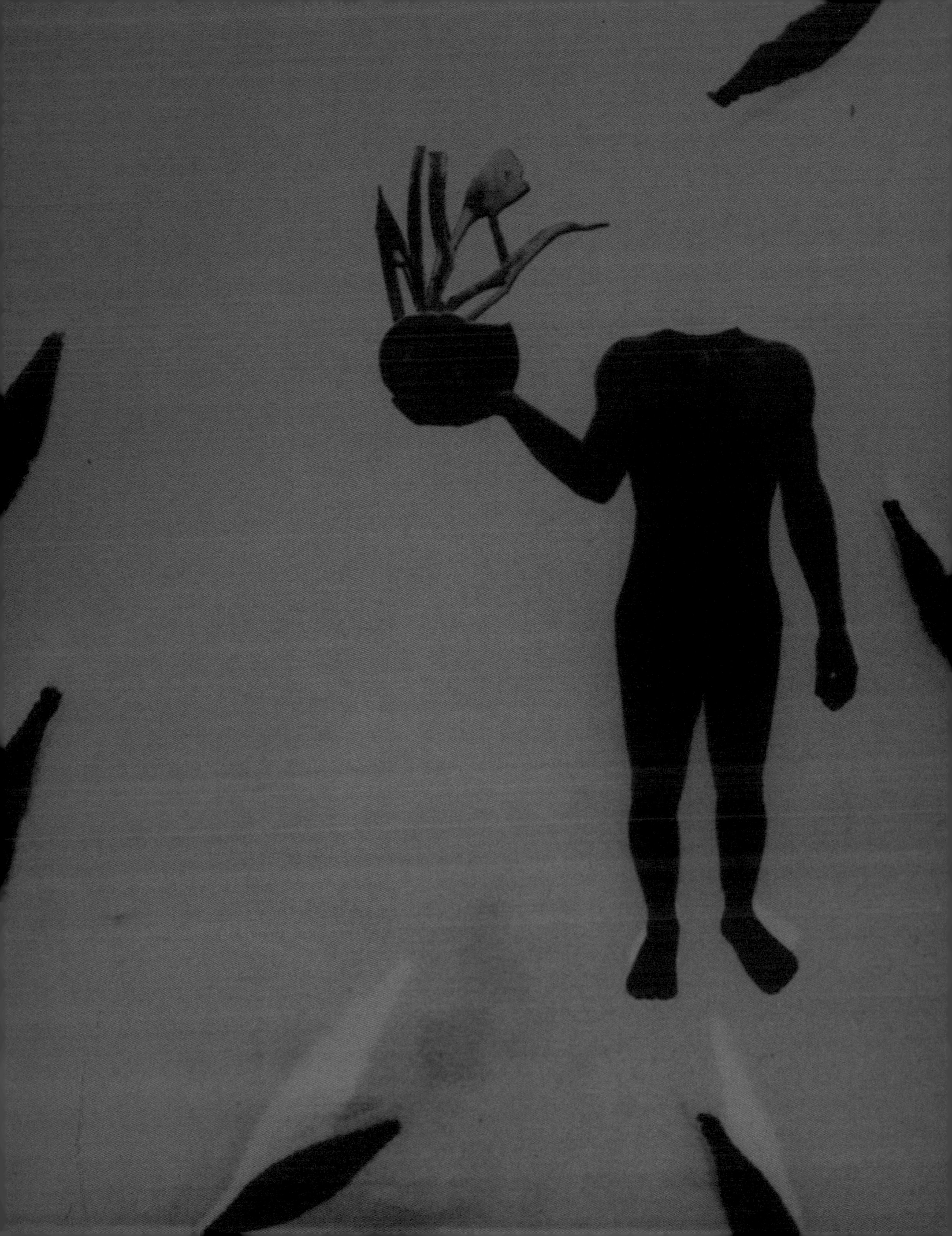

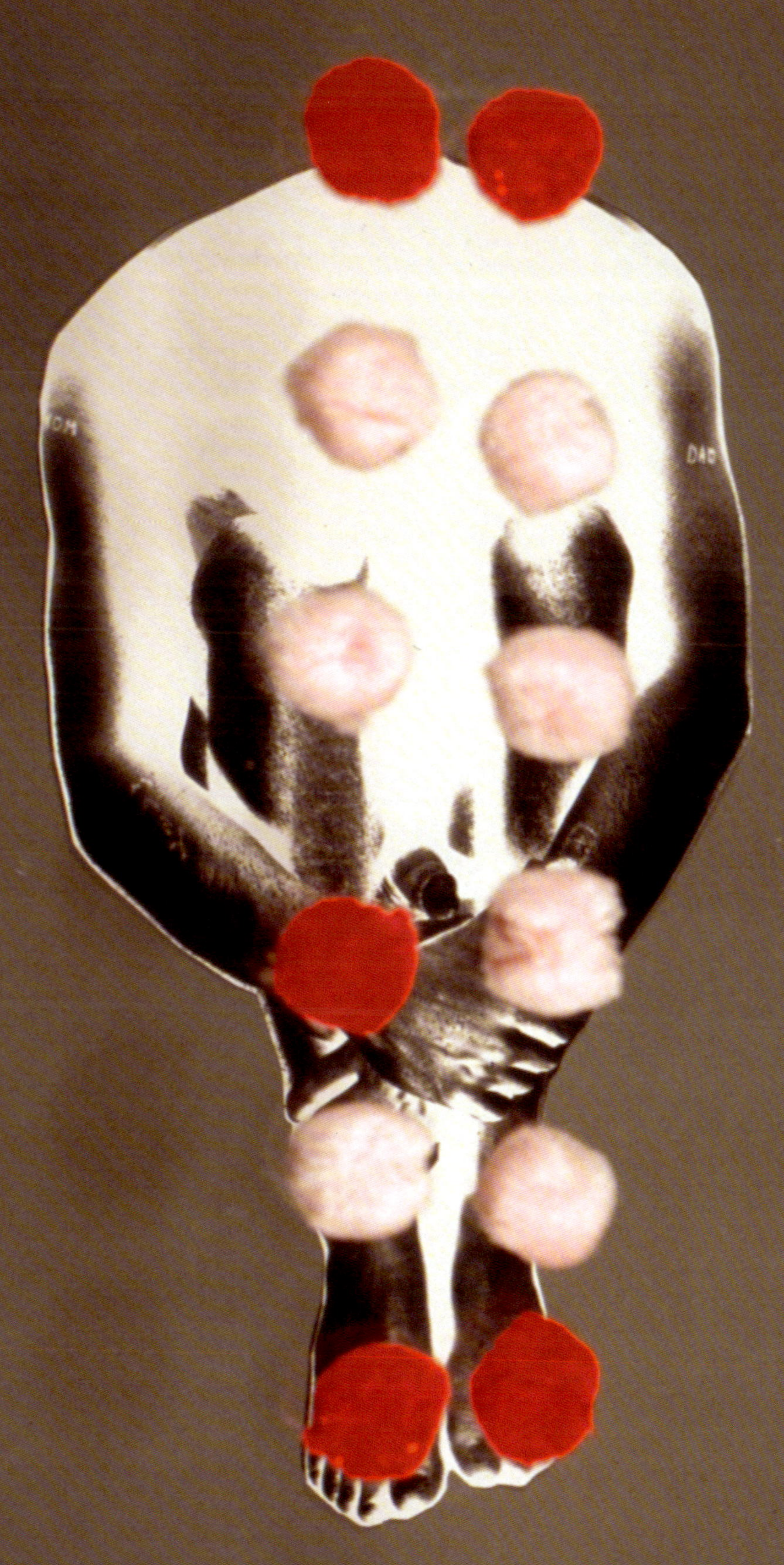
DAD

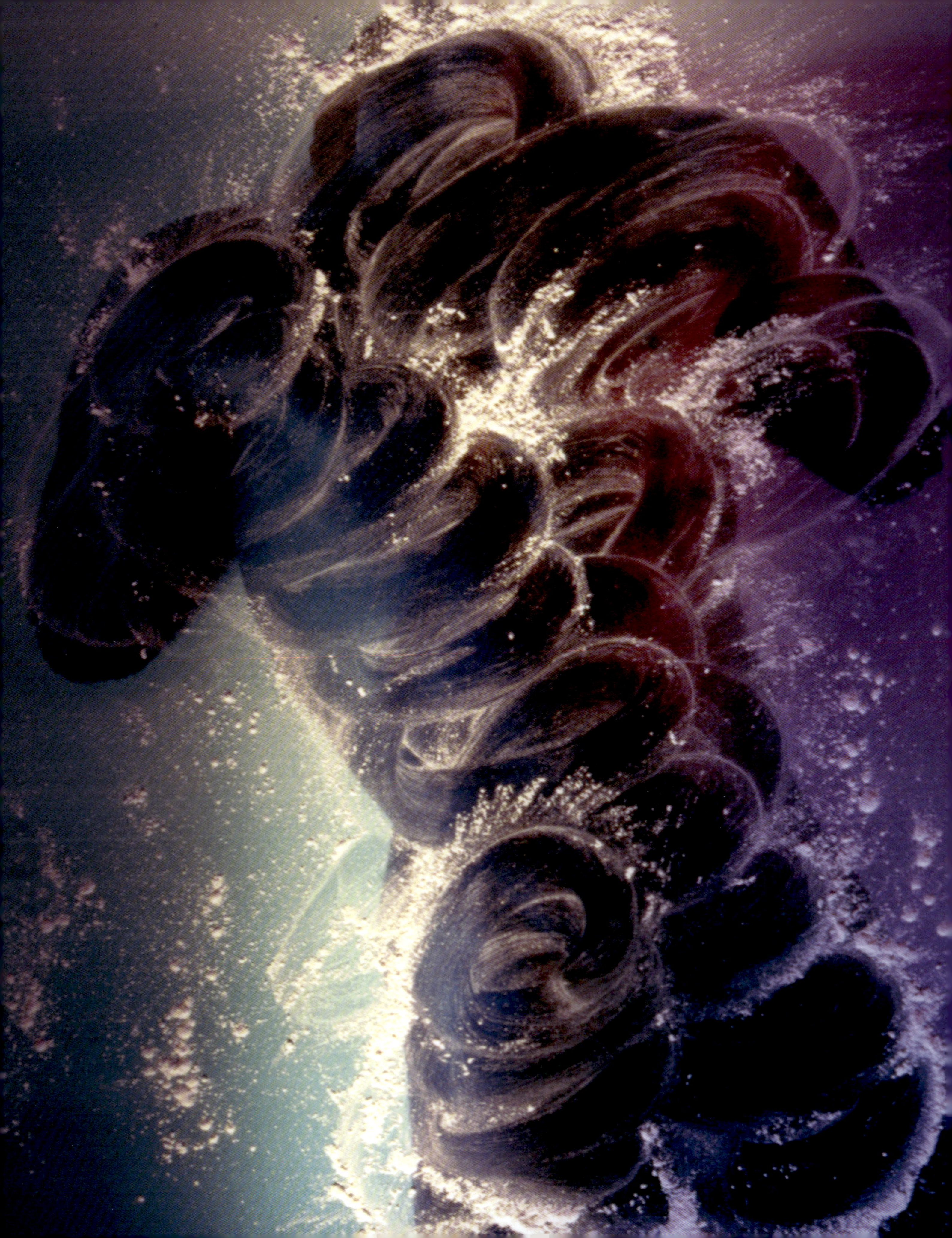

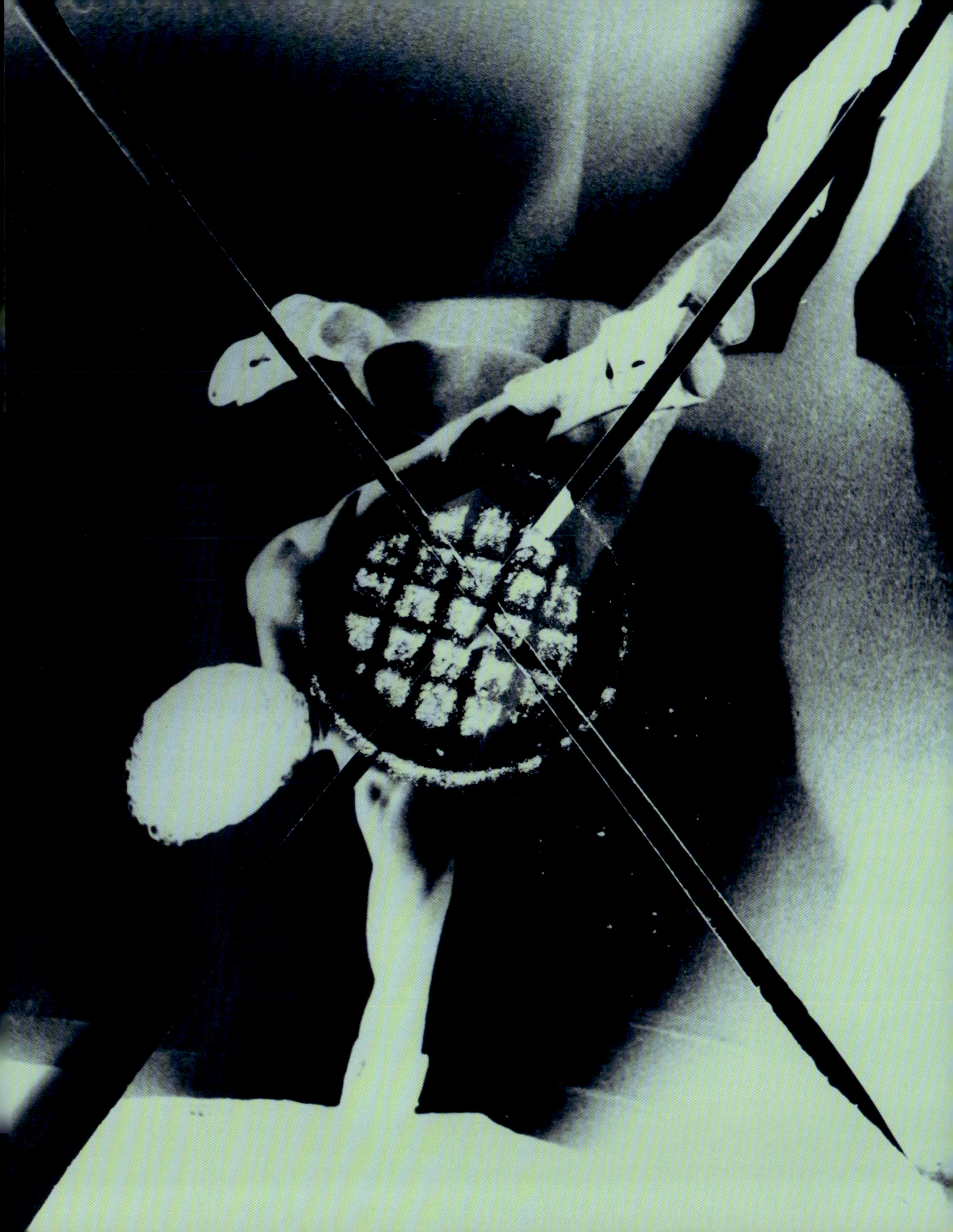

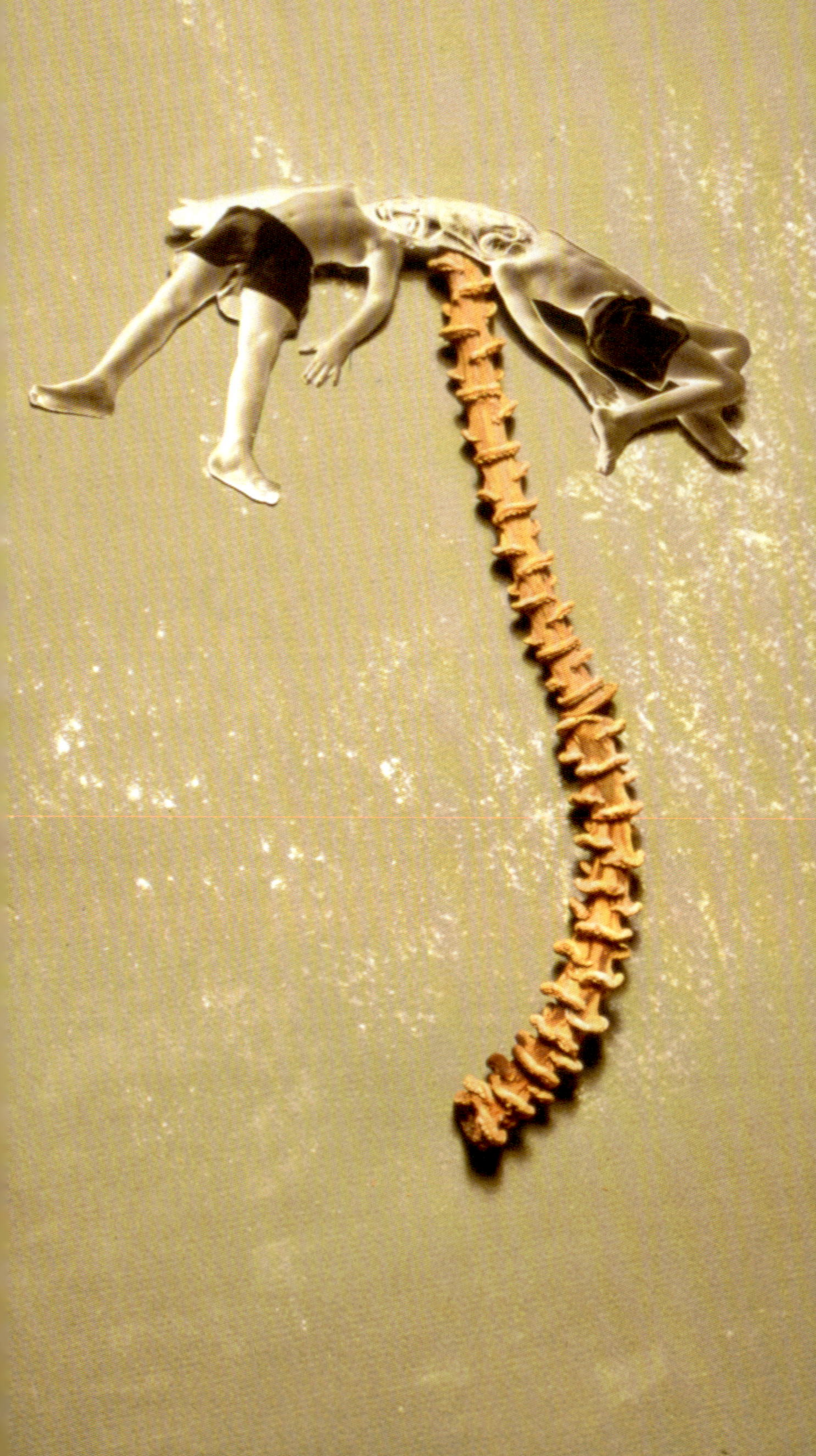

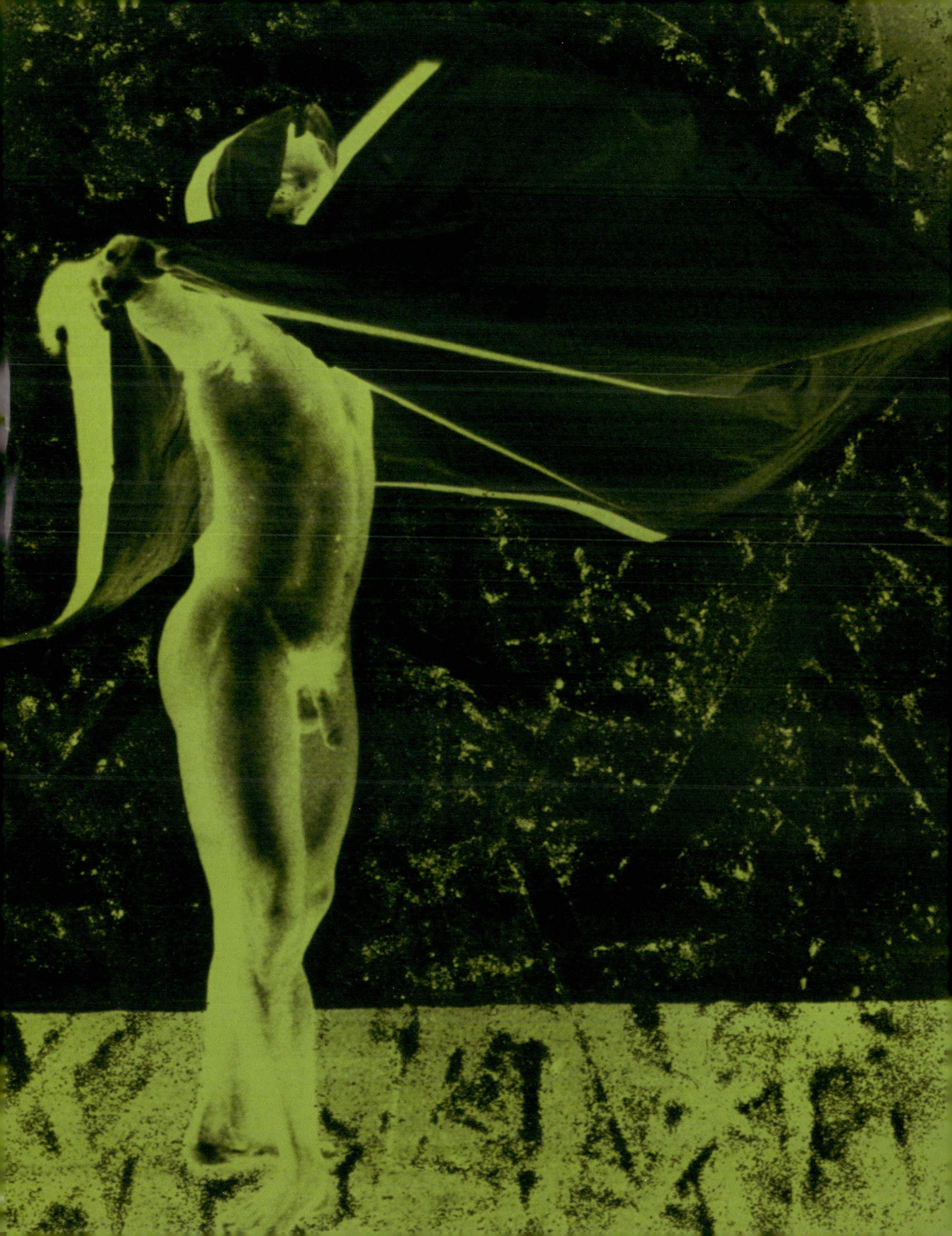

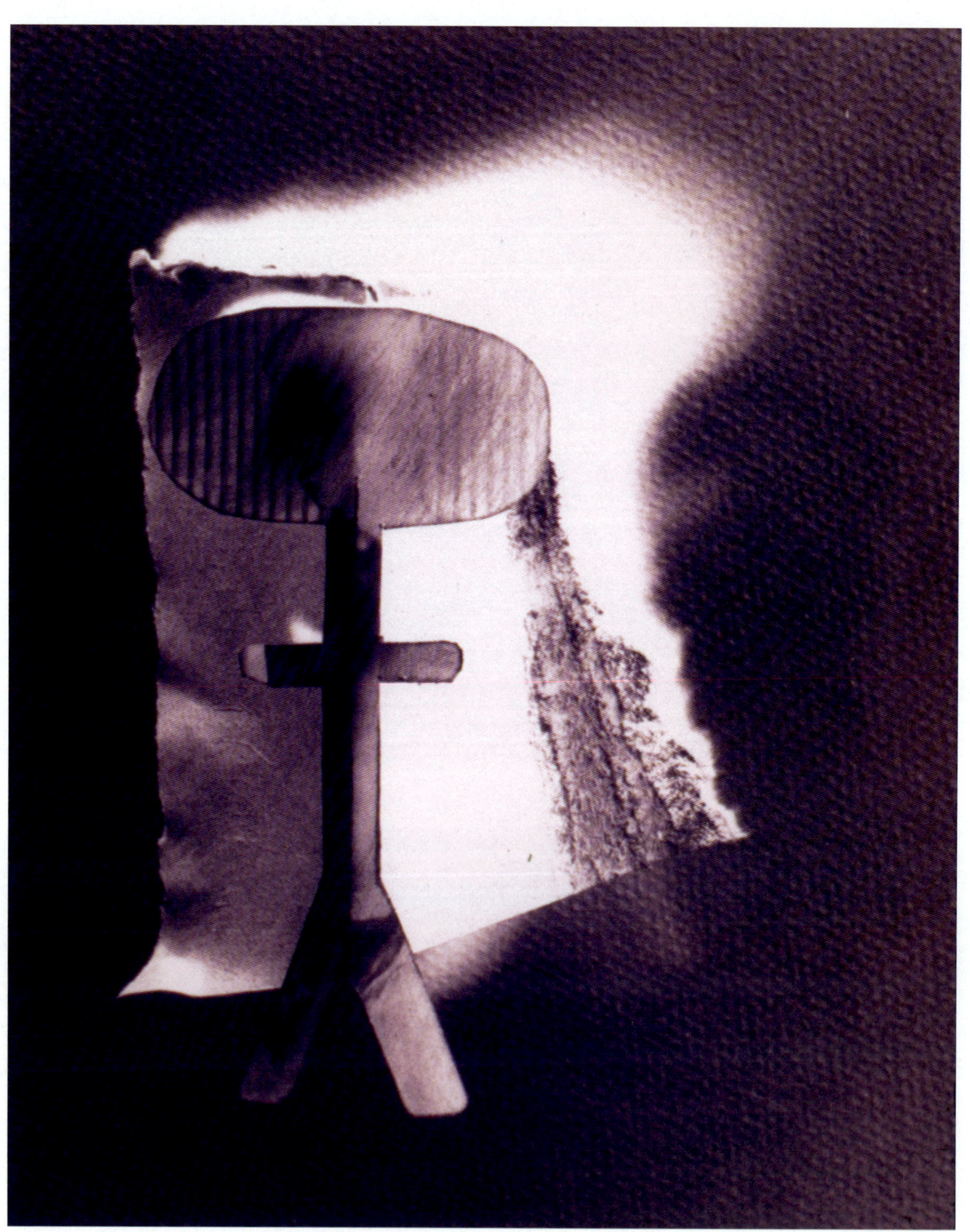

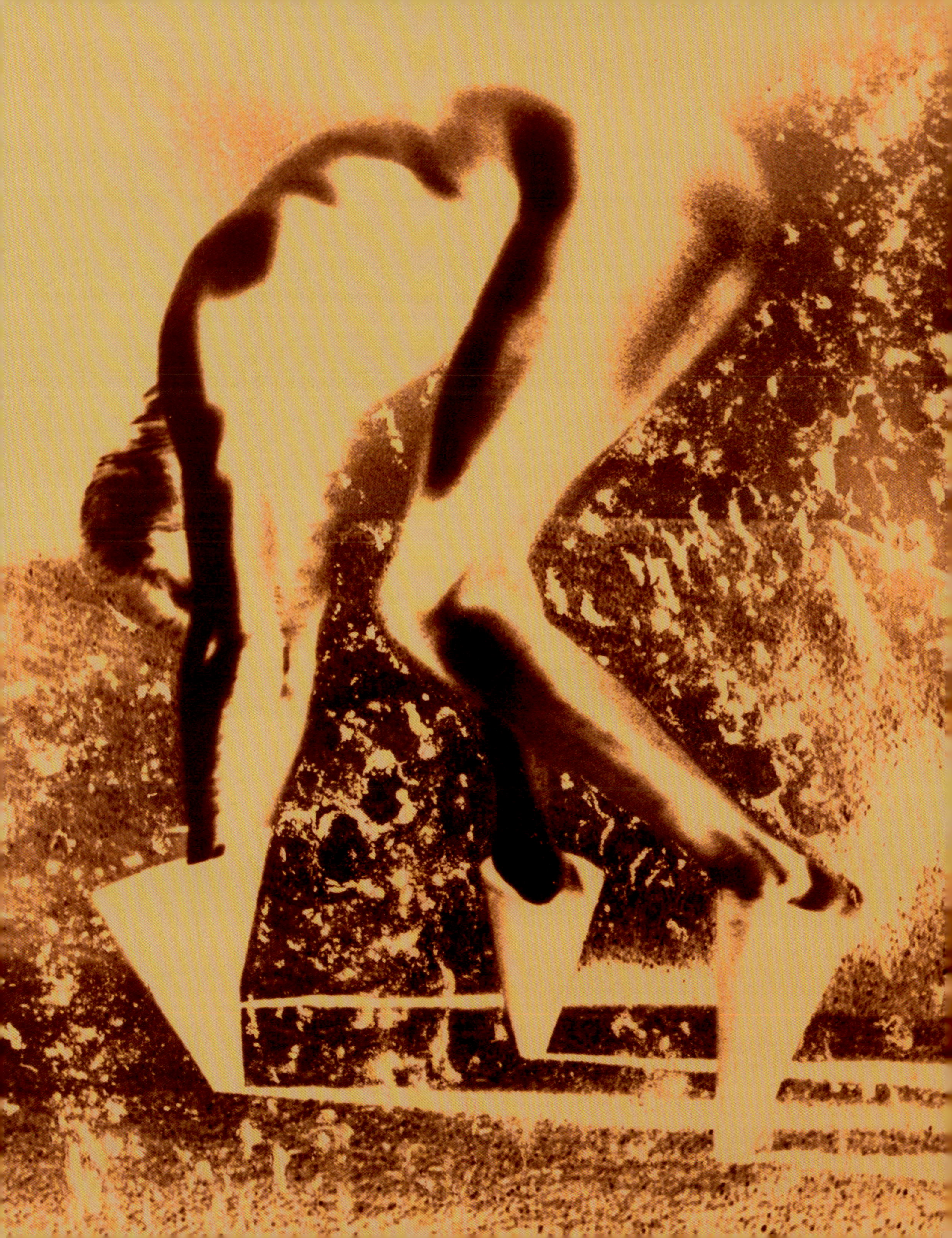

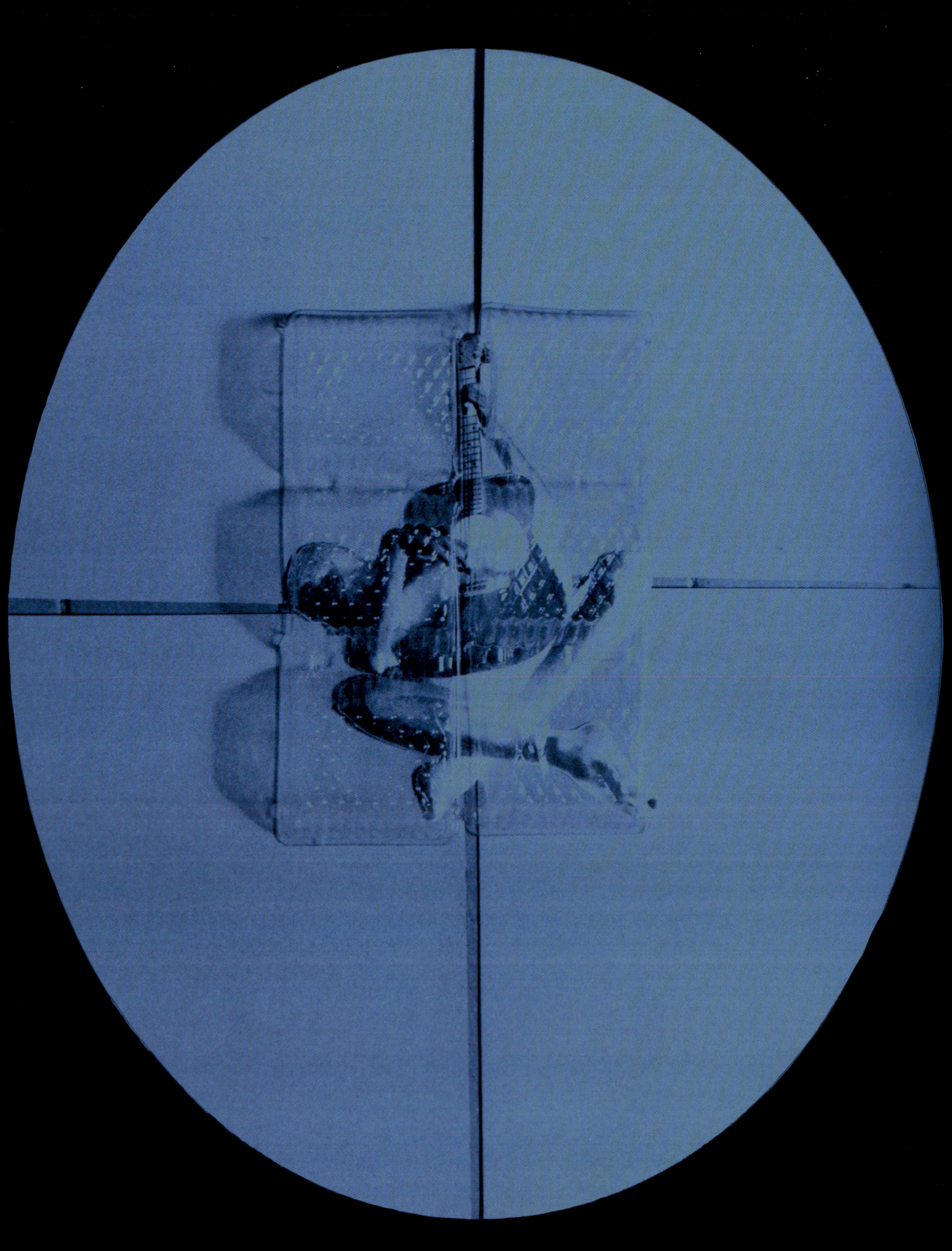

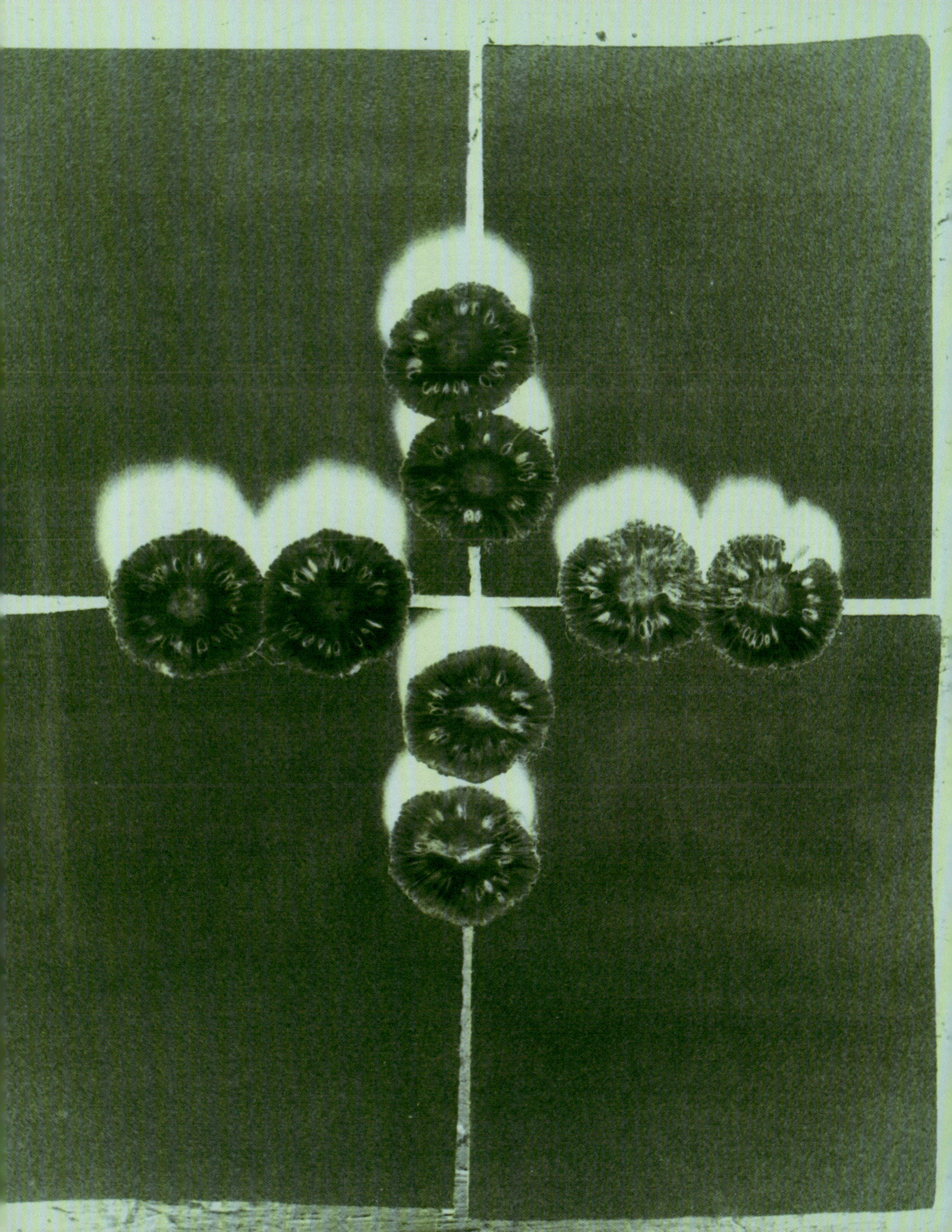

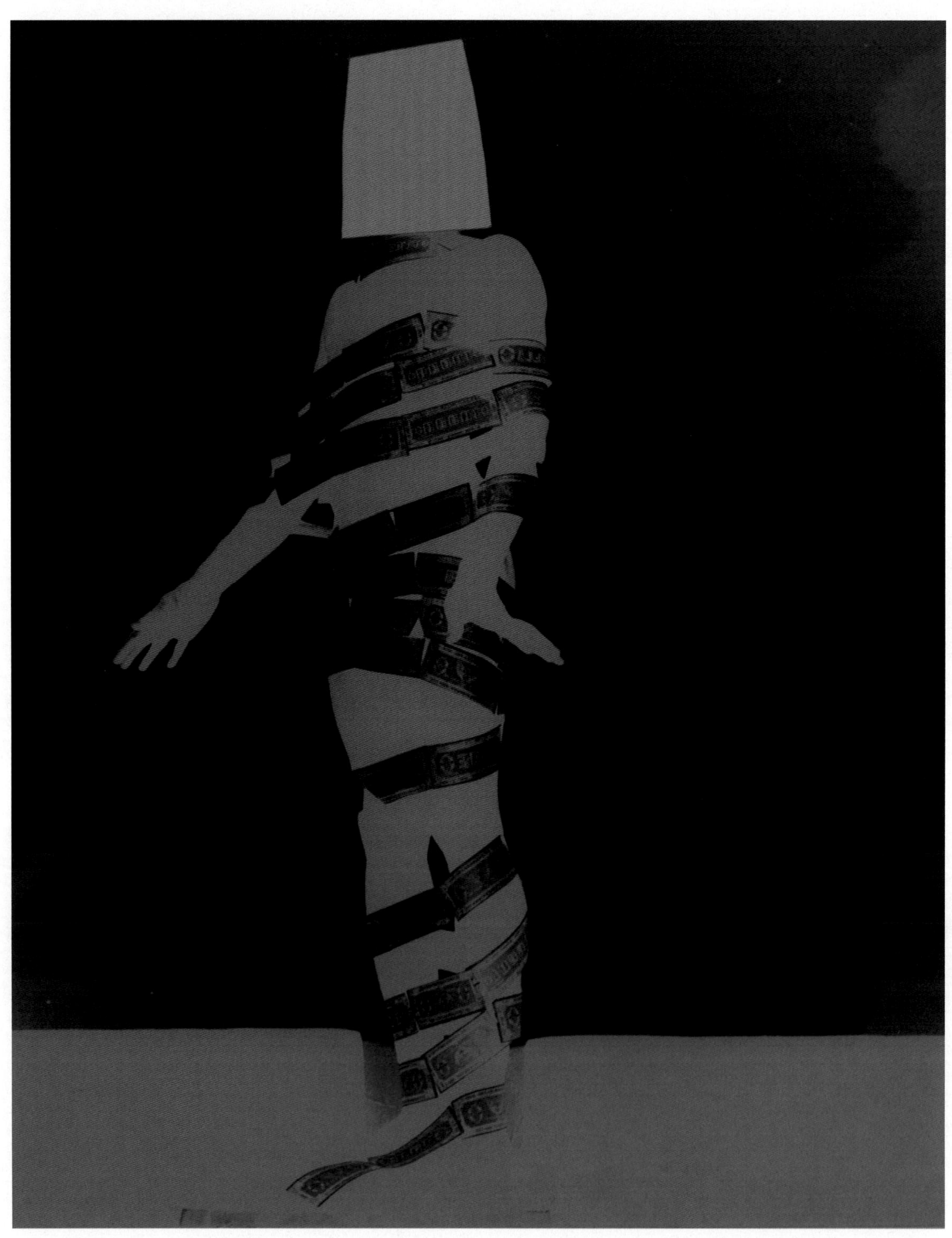

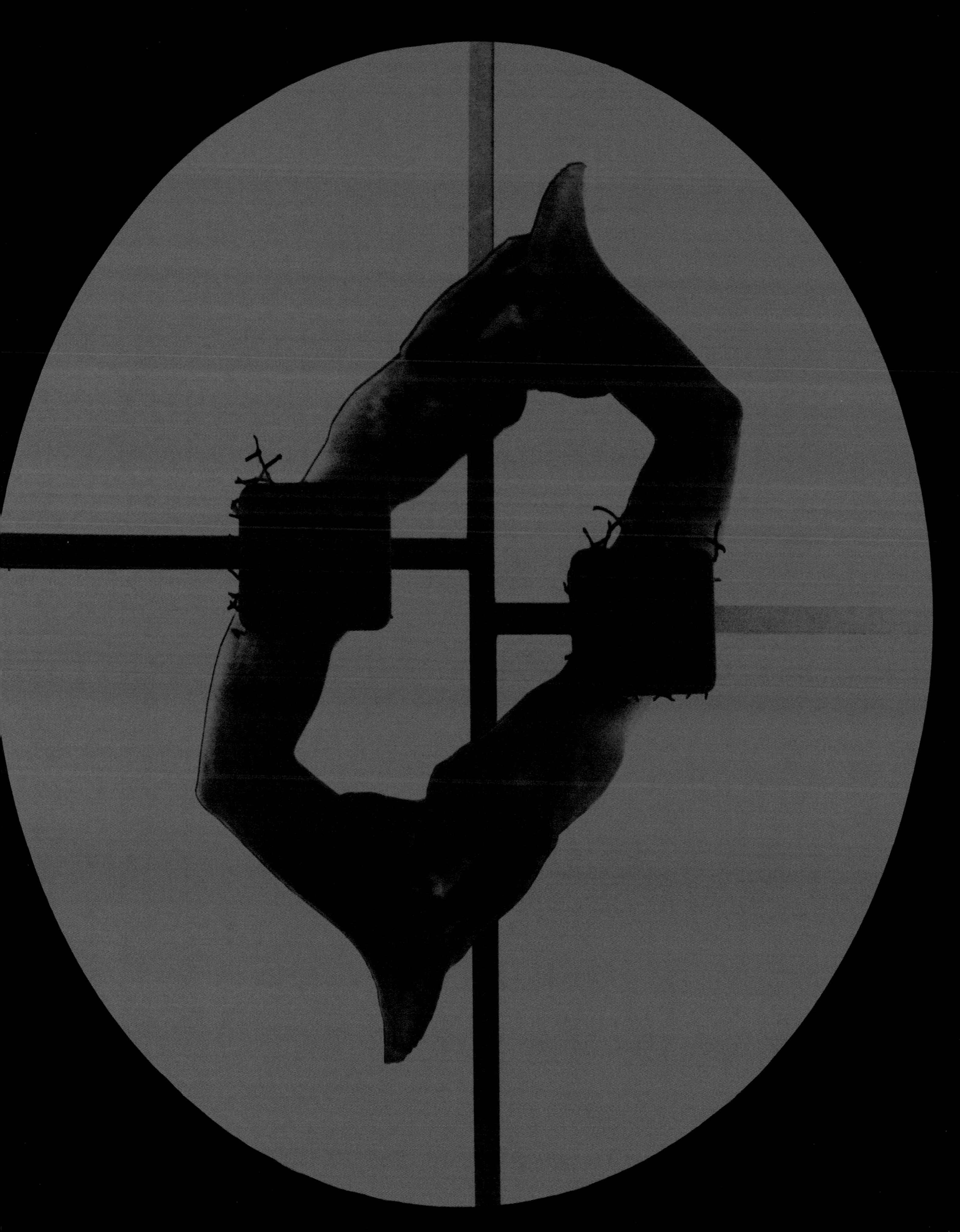

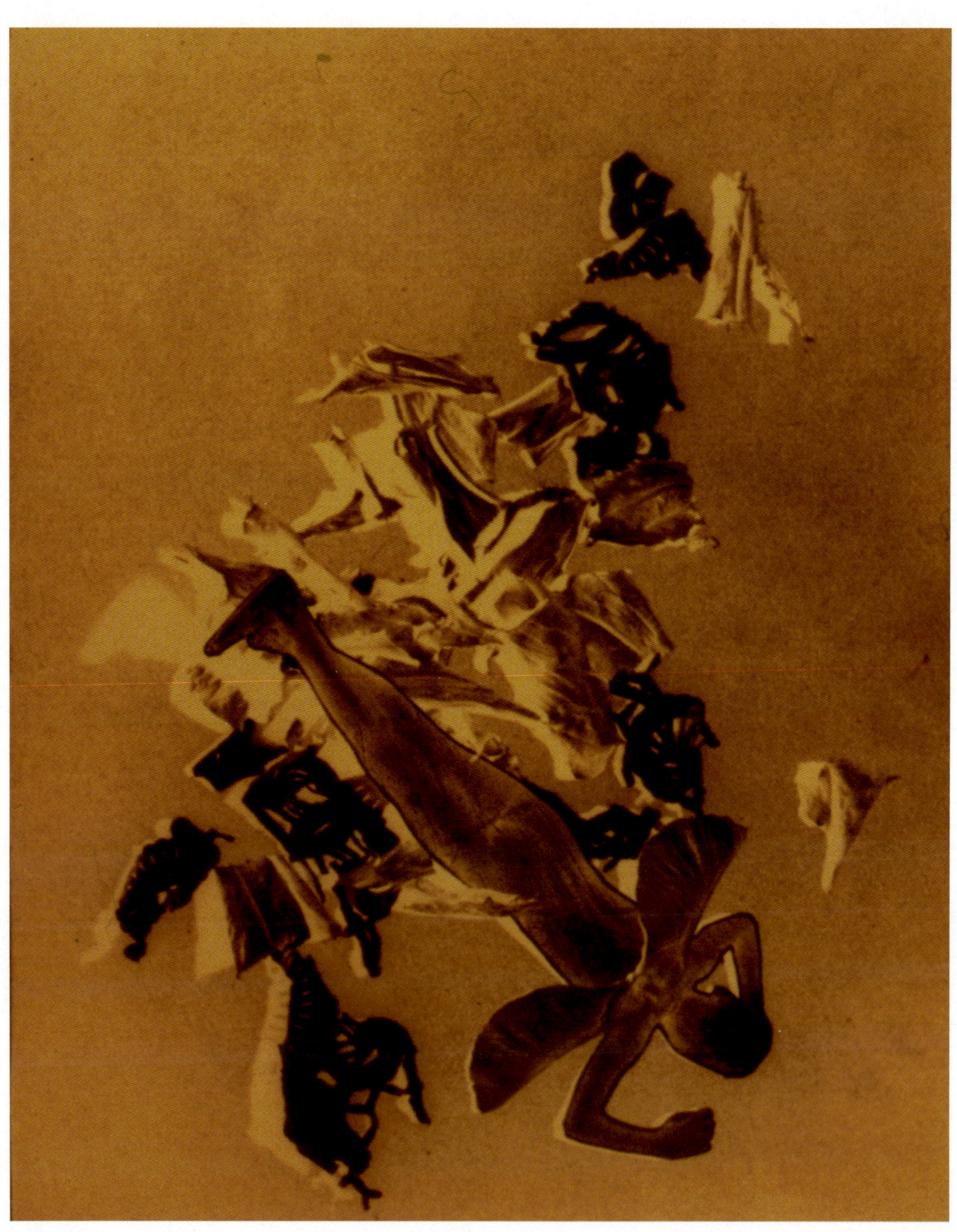

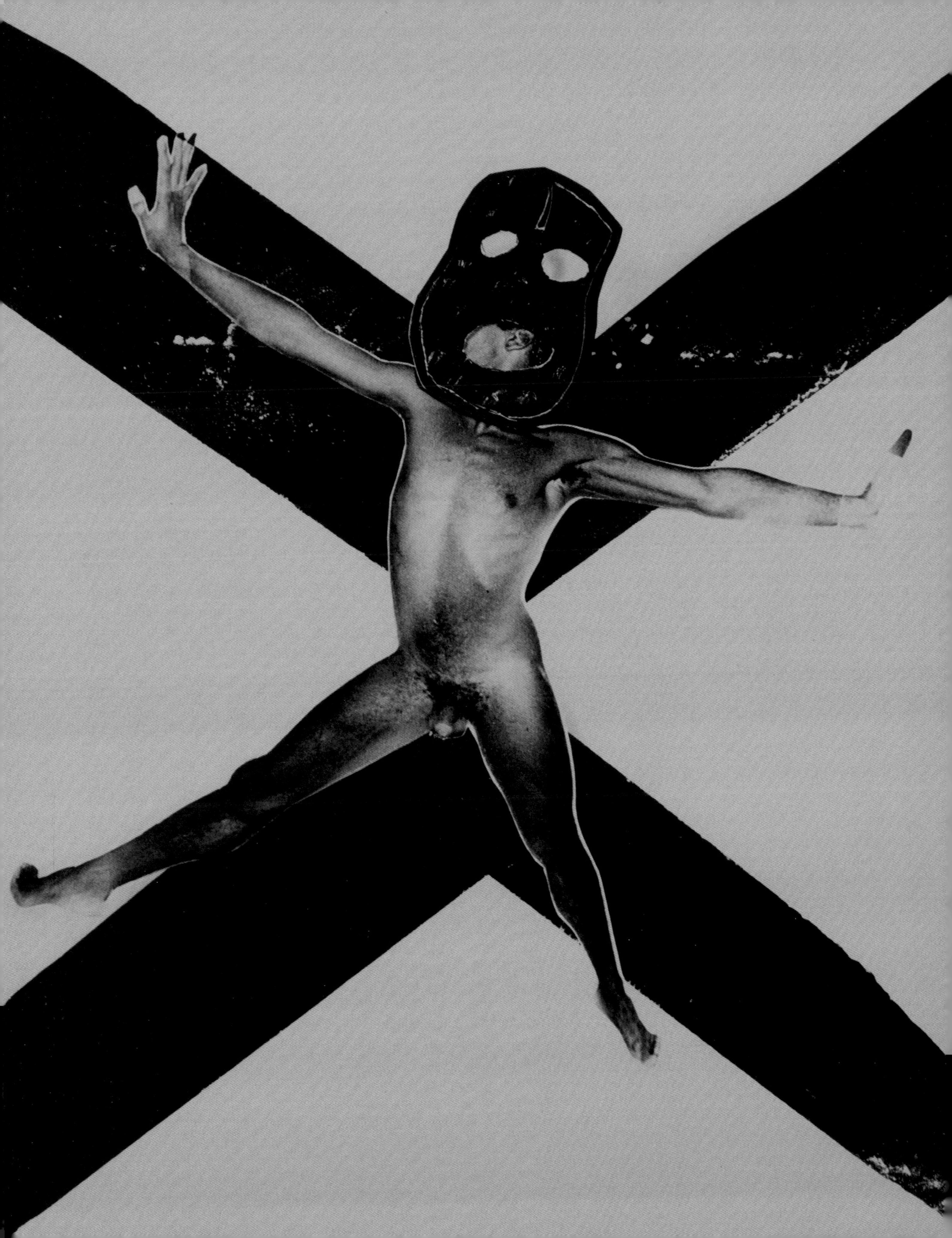

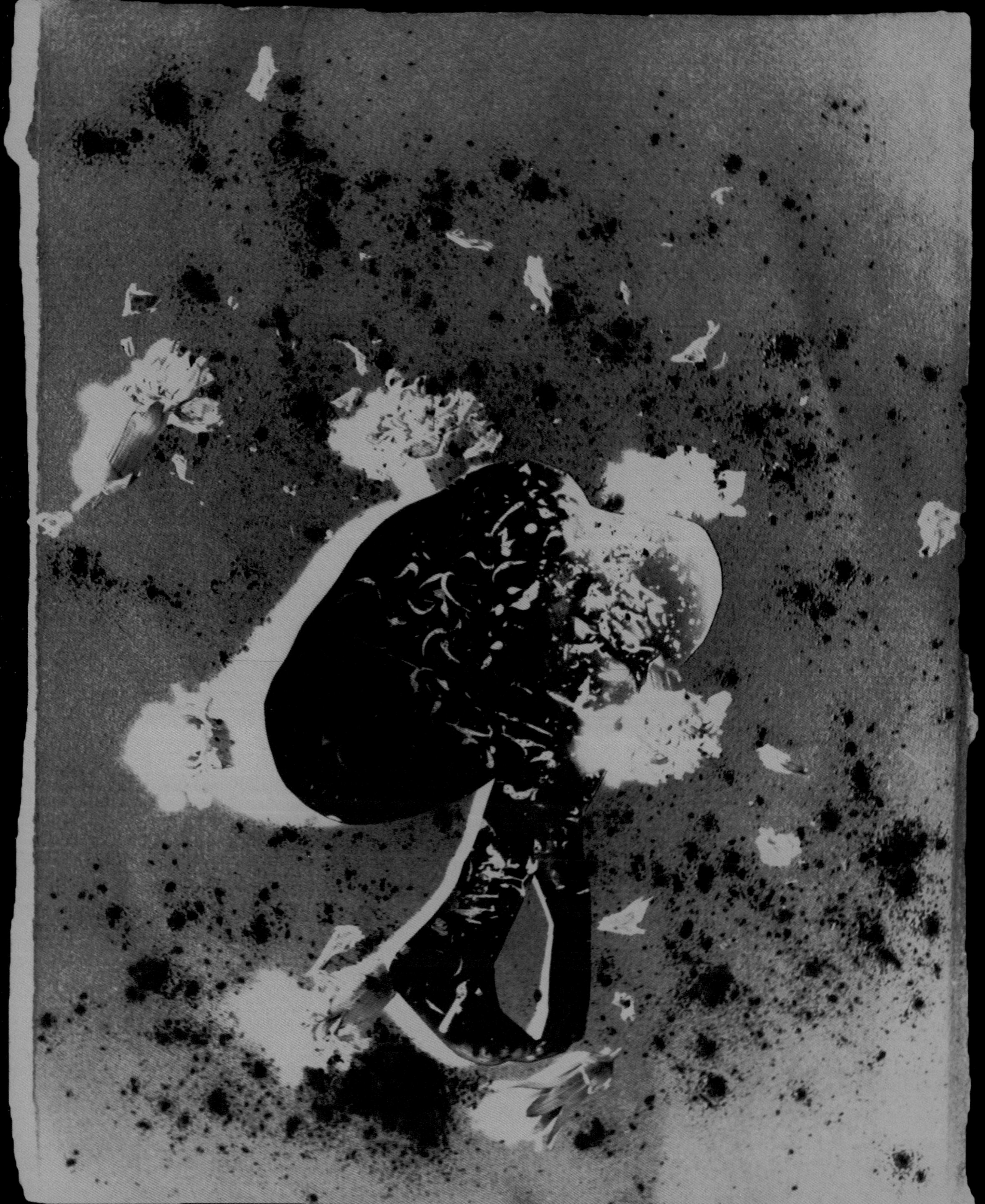

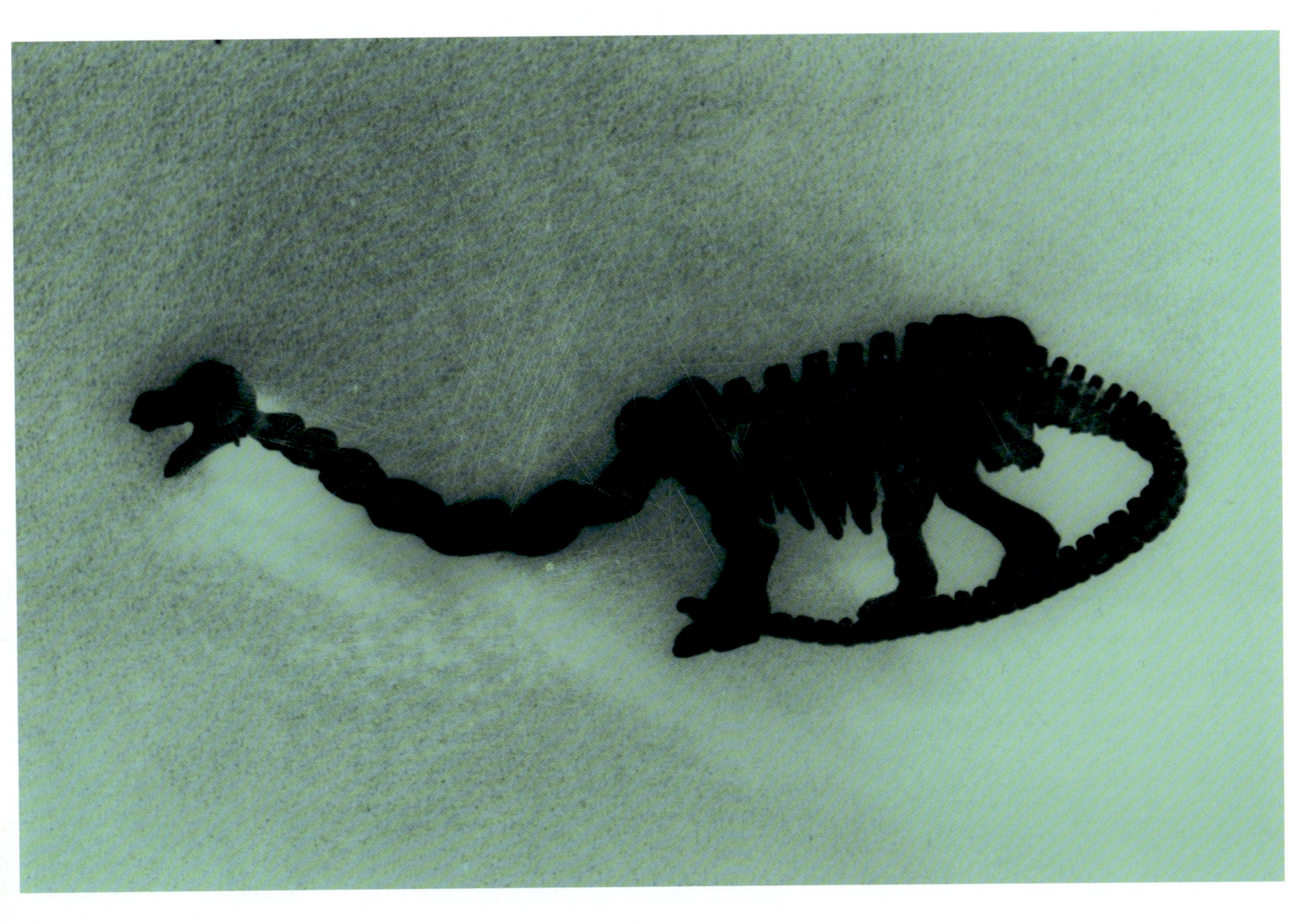

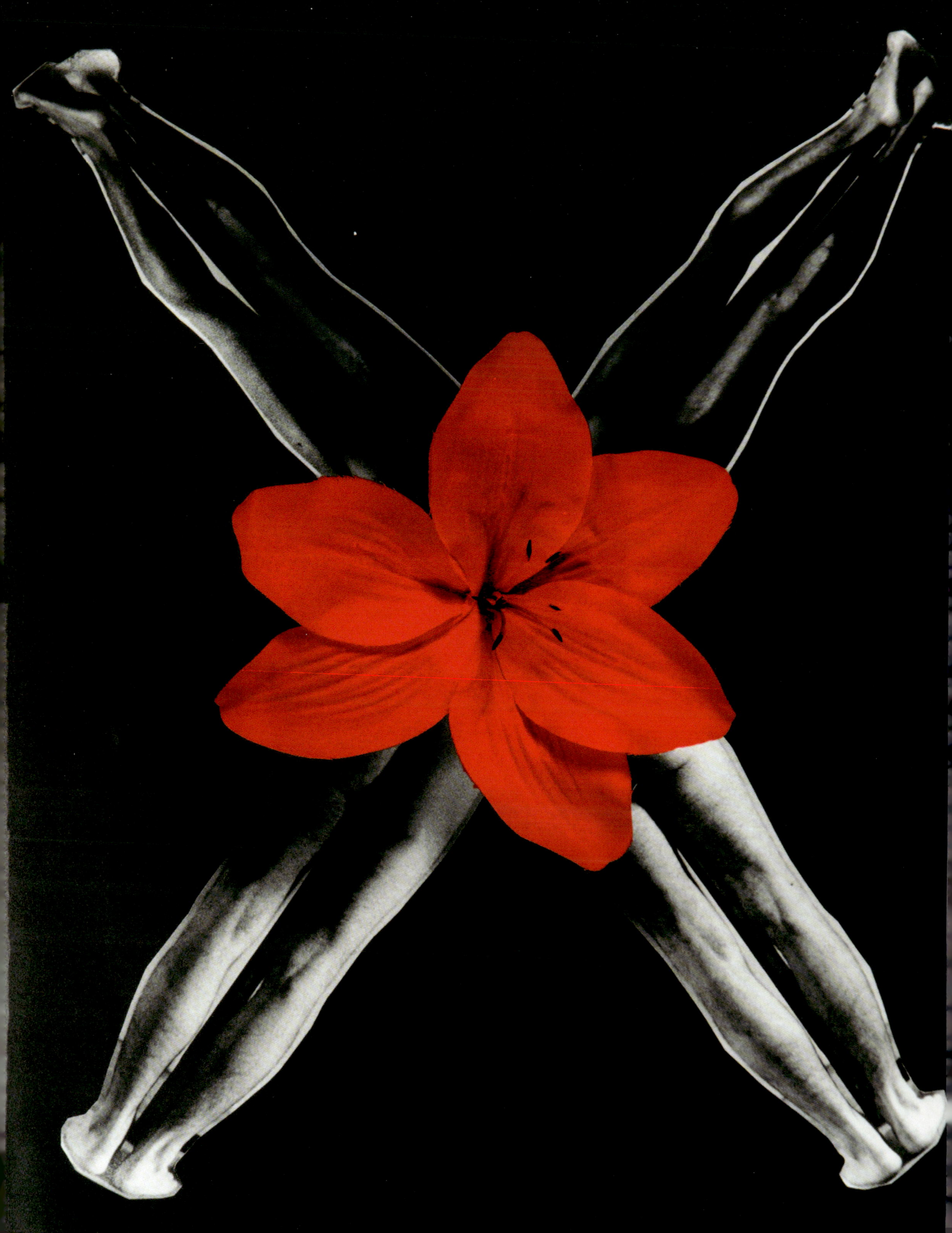

SALVATION

ISBN: 979-8-9885736-3-0

Editors: James Hoff and Laurie Simmons Studio
Designer: Rick Myers

Laurie Simmons Studio is Danielle Bartholomew, Laurie Simmons, and Mary Simpson.

Primary Information
232 3rd St, #A113
The Old American Can Factory
Brooklyn, NY 11215
www.primaryinformation.org

Printed by Musumeci, Quart, Italy

Primary Information would like to thank Isaac Alpert, Gabe Greenberg, and P.P.O.W Gallery.

Primary Information is a 501(c)(3) non-profit organization founded in 2006 to publish artists' books and writings. The organization's programming advances the often-intertwined relationship between artists' books and arts' activism, creating a platform for historically marginalized artistic communities and practices. Primary Information receives generous support through grants from the Michael Asher Foundation, Galerie Buchholz, the Patrick and Aimee Butler Family Foundation, The Cowles Charitable Trust, Empty Gallery, The Ford Foundation, The Fox Aarons Foundation, the Helen Frankenthaler Foundation, Furthermore: a program of the J. M. Kaplan Fund, the Graham Foundation for Advanced Studies in the Fine Arts, Greene Naftali, the Greenwich Collection Ltd, the John W. and Clara C. Higgins Foundation, Metabolic Studio, the New York City Department of Cultural Affairs in partnership with the City Council, the New York State Council on the Arts with the support of the Office of the Governor and the New York State Legislature, the Orbit Fund, the Stichting Egress Foundation, VIA Art Fund, The Jacques Louis Vidal Charitable Fund, The Andy Warhol Foundation for the Visual Arts, the Wilhelm Family Foundation, and individuals worldwide. Primary Information receives support from the Arison Arts Foundation, Willem de Kooning Foundation, the Marian Goodman Foundation, the Henry Luce Foundation, and Teiger Foundation through the Coalition of Small Arts NYC.